Nabokov's Gloves

'Highly literate and intelligent. A real dramatist.' *Guardian*

Iona Rain

'A beautifully crafted work. Moffat's dialogue is tremendous: sparse but rich.' *Independent*

Peter Moffat was born in Edinburgh in 1962. *Iona Rain* was the winner of the International Playwriting Competition in 1995, was nominated for Best New Play in the Writers' Guild Awards, 1996, and was adapted for, and broadcast on, BBC Radio 4. *Nabokov's Gloves* was the winner of the Pearson Television Writers' Award for Best Play of 1997. His first play, *A Fine and Private Place*, was broadcast on BBC Radio 4 in 1997. His other play, *The Blue Garden*, was produced by the Warehouse Theatre, where he was writer in residence. His work for television includes *Kavanagh Q.C.* He is currently writing a new drama series for Channel Four, *EH6*, and a new play for Hampstead Theatre and Associated Capital Theatres, *The Last Soldier*. He lives in north London.

First published in Great Britain in 1999
by Methuen Publishing Limited
215 Vauxhall Bridge Road, London, SW1V 1EJ

Peribo Pty Ltd, 58 Beaumont Road, Mount Kuring-Gai
NSW 2080 Australia, ACN 002 273761
(for Australia and New Zealand)

Methuen Publishing Limited Reg. No. 3543167

A CIP catalogue record for this book is available from the British Library

Papers used by Methuen Publishing Limited are natural, recyclable products
made from wood grown in sustainable forests. The manufacturing processes
conform to the environmental regulations of the country of origin.

ISBN 0 413 77108 6

Typeset by SX Composing DTP, Rayleigh, Essex
Printed and bound in Great Britain by Cox & Wyman Ltd, Reading, Berkshire

Caution

NABOKOV'S GLOVES

&

IONA RAIN

Peter Moffat

Methuen

Contents

Nabokov's Gloves

Nabokov's Gloves was first performed at the Hampstead
Theatre, London, on 14 May 1998. The cast was as follows:

Nick	Greg Wise
Fran	Niamh Cusack
Joe	Dominic Mafham
Martin	David Cardy
Mary	Ruth Gemmell
Darling	Beatie Edney

Directed by Ian Brown
Designed by Robin Don
Lighting by Howard Harrison
Sound by John Owens

Act One

Scene One

Nick *and* **Fran**'s *bathroom.* **Nick** *is looking in the mirror. He is wearing a dark suit. After a short time he turns.*

Nick I don't have much left to say. It's nearly over. But let me ask you something. A question before I stop. What do you see? When you look at me . . . What is the picture? Accent. Suit. Watch. Maybe you've caught a whiff of eau de Givenchy of a morning. Do I see a smile? Have the better noses in the front row taken in an odour . . . of eau de Givenchy? There . . . Yes. Smiles all round. And not just the front row. Such . . . nasal sophistication. High-class nostrils. What else? Maybe some of you have seen me . . . around four thirty, easing out of the car park in my expensive German car. I'm sorry. No need for coyness. It's a Mercedes. It cost thirty-five thousand pounds. Smiles again. Good. So. Expensive accent; expensive car; expensive . . . smell. Expensive . . . expensive . . . expensive. Mr Silky-drawers. It that what you see? Is it? Let me tell you something. Listen. Let me *tell you* something. August 1963. My father left Italy – Genoa – and came here with nothing except me and my mother . . . and his gift. And for twenty years he was a deckchair attendant on the beach at Southend. Twenty years up and down the beach. Singing. Verdi and Puccini and Bellini. He never missed a day's work in twenty years and so Southend – for twenty years, every day – was blessed with his voice. He died the day Margaret Thatcher was elected. Heart attack. In a beach hut. He wasn't found until late in the afternoon. People must have passed by . . . trousers up, Nivea deep, handkerchiefs knotted . . . How long did it take him to die? People must have looked in – the door was open – who were those people who had my father's life in their hands and didn't see or . . . or . . . chose not to see?

The bunting was out in Southend, ice cream was eaten,
Margaret Thatcher was elected and my father died by
himself, in a beach hut, with the fingers of his right hand
trapped in the teeth of a red-and-white striped deckchair.
Now. Do this. It will help. Imagine, God forbid, that
someone you love is arrested, charged and stands trial. Can
you imagine? And let's say it's a serious charge. Why don't
you pick your own? Now. Go ahead. Pick your own charge.
Do you have it? And don't say it couldn't happen.
Remember Guildford? Remember Birmingham? Don't
anyone dare say it couldn't happen. Someone you love . . . in
the dock. His . . . or her whole future in the hands of twelve
people . . . a lot like you . . . perfect strangers, passing by.
Two words for you, members of the jury: sacred task.
Difficult word – sacred – it's losing meaning all the time.
Secularised. Overused. But sacred is the right word, now,
here. And this is your chance to reclaim it and apply it. What
standards would you expect of twelve people trying someone
you love? What standards would you want applied by those
particular passers-by? Sacred task, members of the jury.
Right now this defendant has nothing. You control her life.
You are everything and she is nothing. I've seen juries fail to
look, I've seen juries pass by the open door and I've seen
juries look the other way. Is that you? Or are you something
more? What do I ask from you? I'll tell you. No whims. No
prejudice. Fair minds. Hard, clear thought. Give this woman
the benefit of your clearest and best thought. Give . . . give . . .
fuck it. Fuck . . . it. What is her name? Her fucking name.

Enter **Fran**.

Fran   Hello, darling.

Nick   Shit. Bollocks.

Fran   You could just tape it, once and for all and leave a
blank for the defendant's name. Play the jury a tape. It
would save you energy. I mean . . . it's the same speech.
God knows, it must be getting harder and harder to find the
proper syrup levels after all these years. What's the case?

Nick   Drugs.

Fran   Much?

Nick   Middling.

Fran   When?

Nick   Next week.

Fran   Where?

Nick   Lewes.

Fran   Staying?

Nick   Probably.

Fran   Good.

Nick   Good?

Fran   I mean . . . nice for you. Lewes.

Nick   You don't mind?

Fran   Mind?

Nick   Mind.

Fran   What?

Nick   Me. Fran. Staying. Lewes.

Fran   No.

Nick   You do mind.

Fran   I said no.

Nick   Good.

Fran   Fine.

Nick   Fine.

Fran   Good. How long?

Nick   Week. Mary Duggan.

Fran   The name.

Nick Mary bloody Duggan. You can use a name like that. It's got a tragic . . . something.

Fran Has it?

Nick Like a shipwreck.

Fran A shipwreck.

Nick The *Mary Duggan*. Or a beautiful blind girl from an Irish place with a name. Ballybollybeg. Poor blind Mary Duggan from Ballybollybeg. I could have them weeping over a name like that. A twenty-four-eyed puddle of warm salt water in my gifted palm. Mary Duggan; Mary Duggan. If she doesn't look like a complete hag they'll think she's Joan of Arc by the time I've finished.

Fran Joan of Arc got burnt.

Nick In order to save women like poor Mary Duggan.

Fran Is it poor Mary Duggan?

Nick Oh, I should think so. Provided she's not . .

Fran A complete hag.

Nick Yes. Frankly.

Fran I know what it is. What you do.

Nick Do you, Fran?

Fran Yes.

Nick Are you going to tell me, doctor?

Fran You can hardly wait.

Nick Tenterhooks. Darling.

Fran You're very moved by yourself. You are moving . . . to yourself. You stand in front of the mirror in your beautiful suit – it is beautiful, isn't it? A suit to die in. And you bring yourself to tears . . . often. Regularly.

Nick Is this how it is for your patients?

Fran   Anyway.

Nick   Is that it? Can I unhook my tenters? Doctor? Am I going to live? Can I watch the football later?

Fran   There'll be relics, won't there? Hundreds of years from now. Bone of Pelé. Bobby Charlton's coccyx. A new Turin shroud with Denis Law on it.

Nick   How did you know that?

Fran   What?

Nick   That Denis Law played for Torino?

Fran   I was in the bath. I had just discovered my first grey pubic hair . . . and you came into the bathroom and I told you and showed you and you said: Denis Law's looking a bit grey too. And then we chatted about his Italian period.

Nick   Do you know what I loved about Denis Law?

Fran   Yes.

Nick   The way he pulled his sleeves right down over his wrists.

Fran   Yes, very lovable. An urchin thing. Do you know what I loved about Bobby Charlton? Gorgeous coccyx. Bloody wonderful coccyx.

Nick   Is is Camus again? It this Camus and goalkeeping and everything?

Fran   Albert Camus may have been a goalkeeper once upon a time but he was a fuck sight more interesting in print than he was in six-yard boxes.

Nick   Speech. *J'accuse*. Speech-making. Big fat sentence. Full to overflowing. Speech.

Fran   If Jean-Paul Sartre had been a world-class synchronised swimmer . . .

Nick   Pressing on regardless . . .

Fran   No one would say: oh, Jean-Paul Sartre, friend of
Albert Camus, the goalkeeper, he was a world-class
synchronised swimmer . . . that means synchronised
swimming is fucking marvellous and important as hell and
we should spend all our time talking about it and not talking
to women . . . ever . . . at all.

Nick   Did you write this down first and practice?

Fran   And if Camus had known that he would be single-
handedly responsible for the English middle-class male
backlashing his way to completely acceptable levels of
chauvinism he would never have put on a pair of
goalkeeping gloves in his life.

Nick   'All I know most surely about morality and
responsibility I have learnt from football.' Quote. Unquote.
Albert. And he didn't wear gloves.

Fran   Why do you know that? Why? I cannot imagine
how you come to know that Camus didn't wear gloves.

Nick   Goalkeepers didn't . . . then.

Fran   It's just general then . . . general knowledge about
goalkeepers?

Nick   No. I know specifically that Camus didn't wear
gloves.

Fran   How?

Nick   I don't know. It's why they look a bit crap –
goalkeepers then. They were. They needed gloves, basically.
Even Nabokov needed gloves.

Fran   Nabokov was a goalkeeper.

Nick   Yeah. And no gloves. He would've written
differently . . . if he'd worn gloves . . . in goal. All that flashy
fuck-off prose comes from having sore hands all the time.
He's a sore-handed writer. Fast sentences. Go on, Fran,
have a laugh. A smile maybe. Fran?

Fran It's actually not funny that you prefer football to your wife. It never has been. It's just fucking stupid. Full stop. And just because the little-boy smile leaves us high and dry with an excess of earnestness it doesn't mean we're wrong.

Nick Us? We're?

Fran As you know. Deep down. Good night.

Nick The end?

Fran Yes.

Nick Fran?

Fran Yes?

Nick Terrible eyesight. Sartre. He probably would've banged his head a lot . . . on the bottom of the pool . . . and stuff.

Fran There it is . . . the seeping little-boy smile. End on a joke. The last word.

Nick Probably . . .

Fran What?

Nick Probably they had bad underpants too . . . no gloves and bad underpants. Can you imagine? It was so hard being a goalkeeper. Poor Nabokov. Sore hands and badly arranged genitalia. So hard. The Pope played in goal apparently.

Scene Two

Nick *and* **Joe**'s *room in chambers.*

Nick *puts a tape in the tape-recorder. 'Baby I Love You' – The Ronettes. He listens for a short time and then takes the tape out replacing it with another. He listens intently.*

Policeman   This is your chance to give your side of the story, Mary. Mary? You don't live with anyone, do you?

Silence.

We know you don't live with anyone.

Silence.

So how did it get there?

Silence.

Mary?

Mary (*long pause*)   No comment.

Nick *stops the tape immediately and rewinds it a fraction before replaying* **Mary** *saying No comment. He does the same thing twice more. Then he takes out the tape and replaces it with another – 'Baby I Love You' – The Ramones. He closes his eyes and mouths the lyrics.*

Enter **Joe**. **Joe** *turns the tape off.*

Joe   I'm thirty-two years old. Normal, good character. Articulate. Intelligent. References left, right and centre. Brigadier this, Reverend that, Mrs Blue-rinse the other. They all say I'm splendid. Job, of course . . . and good at it. My whole life in front of me.

Nick   So why?

Joe   I love her. Very simple. I'm in love with her.

Nick   Right.

Joe   I'm the most candid child-abuser of all time.

Nick   How often?

Joe   Three times. Months apart.

Nick   Who?

Joe   Niece.

Nick   Top? Bottom?

Joe   Top, the first two times, a wander downstairs on the third occasion. Not sustained.

Nick   And not under . . .

Joe   Under jeans over pants. Sad fumbles. Tears. You know. And then a roaring conscience.

Nick   Age?

Joe   Twelve. And I want to plead to all three.

Nick   Even the wander downstairs?

Joe   Yes. I know. They'd take top only . . . and top only is so much better. But I'm very frank and it's Gs to all three. Off the chest. All that.

Nick   Helps you really.

Joe   That's what I thought. I could plead guilty to boobs only but I simply refuse to hide from the full and terrible responsibility. I might get the Pros to offer boobs anyway and then despite the offer and as instructed plead to the fanny count too – so I can tell the judge about turning the offer down.

Nick   Who's the judge?

Joe   Some recorder called Gormley.

Nick   You're fucked.

Joe   Really?

Nick   Hates sex.
Any sex. Hates it. He'd have given Humbert Humbert life. Homely Gormley. Never seen his wife with the lights on. Thick as shit. Hundreds of kids. Mention sex and mention niece, twelve, and it's all over. Niece? Twelve? Eighteen months, maybe two years.

Joe   Shit.

Nick   What will it do to you?

Joe   Kill me probably.

Nick   Psychiatric report?

Joe   Too normal.

Nick   Isn't that the point? Can't you get Dr Somebody to say something. Normal isn't normal. A niece is a niece.

Joe   I thought you said . . .

Nick   Yes. I did. Forget it. Take him down. Take down that niece-molester, right now. Can I ask you something?

Joe   I love it when people say that. Sorry, yes. Nicholas. Of course. Ask me something.

Nick   'Baby I Love You'. The Ronettes or The Ramones? Which? Which is definitive?

Joe   Tough.

Nick   But . . .

Joe   The Ramones.

Nick   Because?

Joe   Just . . . because. You know . . . hilarious. Crap. Brilliant. The editor bloke rang.

Nick   Why?

Joe   The brief's changed. He wants short essays. No lists. Essays. Argument. reasons.

Nick   Good. Good.

Joe   That's what I said. And there's more money. They love it. They're chucking money at it . . . and we get . . . quite a lot.

Nick   Any drawbacks? Do they want any . . . control?

Joe   No. Just the title.

Nick   Tell me.

Joe   They want it called 'The Guinness Book of Definitive Versions of Popular songs. Hyphen. 1950 to the Present. Full stop.'

Nick   Two 'ofs'. . . there are two ofs. For fuck's sake. Book of. Versions of. Hideous.

Joe   They said it had gravitas. Long title. Of and of. Makes it sort of . . . definitive.

Nick   Completely hideous.

Joe   Three grand more.

Nick   Right.

Joe   Each.

Nick   Three grand per of.

Joe   Yes.

Nick   The title is OK.

Joe   That's what I said. And essays . . . it's a hell of a compliment.

Nick   'With a Little Help From my Friends'. The Beatles or Joe Cocker?

Joe   Jesus.

Nick   Difficult.

Joe   So difficult.

Nick   But . . .

Joe   No. Can't. Yet.

Nick   We're going to have to.

Joe   I know. Jesus. 'It's in His Kiss'. Betty Everett or Cher?

Nick   Cher. Actually.

Joe   You reckon?

Nick   Yes. I know. Hate to have to say it.

Joe   Why *hate*?

Nick   The old thing – a natural lean to the original.
Sentiment really. You know – older is better, the first cut is
the deepest.

Joe   But Cher, you think?

Nick   Yes. Wall of sound.

Joe   Production.

Nick   And the walking test.

Joe   What?

Nick   Walkman. Very loud. Walk across Waterloo Bridge.
At dawn. Do you swing your arms more to Cher or Betty?
Who does your heart sing along to? Where's the shoop
shoop? And you have to measure the distance. How far
across the bridge you get by the end of the song.

Joe   Wait. You've done this?

Nick   The Cher version is two minutes and forty seconds
long. Betty's is ten seconds shorter. Eight lamp-posts with
Cher . . . five only with Betty. Quicker walk with Cher . . .
it's the better version. It's a good test. It's applied
mathematics.

Joe   You actually did this?

Nick   You're going to have to take this more seriously,
Joe. I mean, laboratory conditions have to be right. You
can't just sit on some sofa at nine thirty *a.m.* or something . . .
on a Tuesday . . . eating Ambrosia Creamed Rice or
something and expect to . . . you need light feet and not
much belly.

Joe   Or something.

Nick   I should tell you something, Joe. It's a bit weird.

Joe   You can tell me. I'm your best friend.

Nick   The last test . . . on Waterloo Bridge. 'Walk On By'. I saved it for the last because it was the easiest.

Joe   Very easy.

Nick   Very. It's a long song. Three and a half minutes. But with Dionne . . . listening to Dionne . . .

Joe   Yes?

Nick   It's very weird. When the song ended . . . when I stopped walking and came back to the world . . .

Joe   What?

Nick   I was at Elephant and Castle.

Joe   In three and a half minutes.

Nick   I know. I think I flew. There are songs you can fly to, Joe. There are songs that are hundreds of lamp-posts short. And actually . . . scares the hell out of you . . . I mean . . . there are people . . . give them a Walkman and the right music . . . with me it was Dionne Warwick, but for other people it's 'Land of Hope and Glory' . . . and for some people it's 'Tomorrow Belongs to Me'. You can get from Waterloo Bridge to Poland on the right song.

A silence. **Nick** *sighs.*

Joe   My God. You did, didn't you? You sighed. That was a sigh. I've never known you sigh outside of Upton Park. So. Sighing all of a sudden. Nicholas.

A silence.

Nick   And then silence. The witness will always fill the silence if you wait long enough.

A silence.

The courage to wait.

A silence.

It's a client.

Joe   Right. A client. Jesus.

Nick   I didn't say I'd . . .

Joe   What?

Nick   Slept with her or anything.

Joe   Or anything. Does Fran know?

Nick   No. She doesn't know.

Joe   You're going to do it, aren't you?

Nick   I don't know. Probably. Yes.

Joe   Who is it?

Nick   Mary Duggan.

Joe   Mary Duggan.

Nick   Yes. Mary Duggan.

Joe   What? Like I should know her? Mary Duggan. Let me guess. Irish?

Nick *shakes his head.*

Joe   Scots?

Nick *nods slightly.*

Joe   Desperately sad-eyed. Thin-limbed. Pale. Freckles to break your heart.

Nick   She's a small-time drugs dealer living in Brighton. Allegedly.

Joe   But Scots?

Nick   They moved down to Sussex when she was a child.

Joe   But Scots.

Nick   Yes.

Joe   Waif.

Nick   Yes.

Joe Sad-eyed.

Nick All right.

Joe Freckles.

Nick Pale. Too.

Joe A Scots lassie away from home. And is that the most terrible sadness in her sad Celtic faraway sad eyes? Does she pine, the lassie, for bonnie bonnie everything? And is that Harry Lauder hand in hand with Moira Anderson somewhere in the gloaming way way back behind her sad sad faraways? And does she remember Jinking Jimmy Johnstone? Did her daddy take her once upon a time to Hampden Park and up on his shoulders did she see the wee man? So small. So pale. So thin-limbed. So freckled. And so . . . gifted. Brings a tear to the eye. Does she use needles?

Nick No.

Joe Have you checked?

Nick What is this?

Joe Have you?

Nick I spent a whole hour and a half looking at her arms. She wore a white T-shirt. And she put her arms on the desk . . .

Joe And?

Nick And nothing.

Joe What do you mean 'she put her arms on the desk. And nothing?'

Nick Just that.

Joe You're in love with her arms. No. Worse than that. You're in love with the way she puts her arms on the desk. So tell me. What's so marvellous about the way she puts her arms on the desk?

Nick   She . . . places them. Like something she cares for. Grace. Slow grace.

Joe   And you went home and listened to Van Morrison long into the night.

Nick   How do you know that?

Joe   Celtic camp. Cheap Yeats. Your cup of tea.

Nick   I knew you'd help. Thanks.

Joe   Pleasure. It wasn't help you were after, though.

Nick   No.

Joe   You wanted to say her name a lot.

Nick   Shall we have a drink?

Nick *gets a bottle of champagne from the fridge.*

Joe   You can just go ahead and say it if you want.

Nick   What?

Joe   You can just . . . say her name . . . if you like. You don't even have to put it in a sentence. I won't mind.

Nick   All right.

Joe   Go on then.

Nick   All right. I can't now.

Joe   You know you want to.

Nick   Of course I want to.

Joe   Are you scared?

Feeling like a fool? Or a fucking idiot, Nick?

A silence.

Not just the arms then?

Nick   No. Everything. Fingers. Everything. And grace. She has real grace.

Joe Grace is . . .

Nick Something . . .

Joe Yes. We'd better drink some more. We'd better drink bottles and bottles.

Nick Where are you tomorrow?

Joe Bow Street. Old-style in a murder, actually. Since you ask. It's all right – pour away.

Nick *pours more champagne.*

Joe Completely bollocks submission. I could do it pissed and stand no worse chance of getting out. I think I will do it pissed, actually. Client's a prat . . . with a charmed life. I've got him off three street robberies in three years. Very guilty every time. Not a word of thanks. Of course.

Nick Of course not.

Joe Gary Mills just . . . gets off. It's his *right* to get off.

Nick Absolutely.

Joe And now he's graduated to the big M. He thinks he's untouchable, thanks to me. He's decided to start killing people. I've kept Mr Mills free to stick six-inch knives in people's stomachs. In a pub garden . . . on a Sunday lunchtime in Lancaster Gate, for fuck's sake. For . . . what? For being there . . . basically. Oi. You. Looking at me? Are you? You fucking looking at me? Blonde-pussy-cunt fucker. You want some? Here you are then. Have a bit of this. Dead. Arrested fifteen minutes later, three streets away, ordering some Kentucky Fried Chicken. Gary Mills. What a good job I've been doing. Three street robberies. That's what? Four grand? Paid for my week in Rome. I lay on my back with an Italian girl whose name I couldn't pronounce and looked at the ceiling of the Sistine Chapel – awestruck – while Gary Mills' victim lay on his back in Lancaster Gate with a knife in his stomach . . . awestruck. That's the equation. Not guilty. Not guilty. Not guilty. Roman holiday.

Blonde-pussy-cunt fucker. Dead. Was I in Rome or was I in
Lancaster Gate?

Nick   Not now, Joe.

Joe   Oh yes. Sorry. Love not death. Much more
important.

Nick   Only a job, Joseph. The system works. It's the only
question. Does it work? If the answer if yes – shut the fuck
up and get on with it.

Joe   Simple.

Nick   Like taking candy from a baby.

Joe   Once you're in, you're in.

Nick   Exactly. Anyway – aren't you going to ask me
more?

Joe   Anyway no. I want to concentrate on your stupidity.
How long have you . . .

Nick   I've had two conferences. Yesterday and the day
before. I've got another one tomorrow.

Joe   Three cons.

Nick   Yes.

Joe   In four days. With a small-time drugs dealer. You've
decided to go public then? How are you going to justify it to
the Legal Aid Board? Love? Love on Legal Aid? Do the
clerks stick that in the diary. Love conference. Five p.m.
What are you going to put in the Note for Taxation? This
was a particularly difficult case owing to the fact that I was
in love with the lay client. It was necessary, in the interests
of justice, to lay the lay client. I request payment
commensurate with the size of my feelings for the said lay
client. And, Nicholas, what do the clerks say about three
cons with Ms Waif?

Nick   They understand.

Joe   They *know?*

Nick   Martin knows.

Joe   God.

Enter **Martin**.

Talk of the devil.

Martin (*to* **Nick**)   You're a cunt. Sir.

Joe   Hello, Martin.

Martin (*to* **Nick**)   You're a total cunt.

Joe   Sometimes I feel so old and wise and full of language skills it breaks my heart.

Martin   And you're a cunt too – listening to him.

Joe   Well, that's the three of us then. Two cunts and the devil.

Martin   Yeah. And I'm a cunt for letting him fuck about.

Joe   Three cunts then. Let's just call it three cunts.

Martin   All over a Doris.

Joe   A Doris called Mary.

Martin   Three cunts over a Doris called Mary.

Joe   Honestly. Us boys. Aren't we the ones? Drink, Martin? You're looking a bit sober for a senior clerk at the end of the day.

Nick   Bottle's finished.

Joe   Martin.

Martin   Fine.

He starts to go but stops at the door.

Joe   Oddbins is waiting.

Exit **Martin**.

How much does he earn?

Nick Hundred and fifty. Officially.

Joe Terrifying.

Nick But we couldn't do without him.

Joe No.

Nick He's all heart.

Joe Absolutely. All heart.

Joe I've been thinking.

Nick Yes.

Joe About death-row work and going to Texas.

Nick Yes.

Joe We should do it. We should just go and do it.

Nick Ankles.

Joe What?

Nick Profoundly beautiful ankles.

Joe I've just decided . . . I'm not your friend any more.
Find another best friend. I've got work to do.

Nick You said it was a bollocks submission.

Joe Less bollocks than this bollocks. Less bollocks than
ankles. Give me a murder, any time. Love can go and . . .
death is better. Drink with Martin. Spend the night with
him . . . that might . . . I don't know. Get your tear ducts
going – the two of you. Do some favourite moments
together. You be Barry Davies and get Martin to sing
'Nessun Dorma' and then tell each other exactly what you
were doing when those penalties were missed and then keep
hold of all that feeling and think about Fran . . . very hard.
Get very tearful, hug Martin in some desperate gutter and
think of Fran.

Nick Joe.

Joe Yes.

Nick We're a bit . . . you're a bit like me. I mean, you understand . . . a bit.

Joe A bit.

Exit **Joe**. *Some moments later enter* **Martin** *carrying three bottles of champagne.*

Nick Three.

Martin One each. Where is he?

Nick Working.

Martin He gets all lary and . . . 'Oddbins is waiting' and then he fucks off.

Nick He's got that murder committal.

Martin Mills. Right. That's tomorrow. Bit of a worry.

Nick Why?

Martin Solicitor says it could go tomorrow. Fuck-all evidence. Bit of a worry. Last thing we want is a decent murder going down the plughole in the Magistrates Courts. Worth twenty grand, silk and junior, if it goes all the way. Turns into one pound fifty if Mr 'Oddbins is waiting' persuades the muppets in the Mags there's no case to answer. We should have kept him drinking. I mean, he wanted the bloody stuff, he should drink it. Yeah? Sir? Nick?

Nick Yeah.

Martin Is he still in chambers?

Nick Yes.

Martin Right. I'll get him.

Nick   He's better . . . in court . . . when he's hungover.
Goes all quiet and bashful and boyish and people want to
look after him. He's better when he's hungover.

Martin   So we should leave him. Leave him sober.

Nick   Don't worry, leave Joe alone. You'll get your trial
and ten per cent of whatever to add to your colossal
earnings. Who's the solicitor?

Martin   Barry Hughes.

Nick   Barry Hughes. Barry Hughes. If I was in trouble I'd
rather have my gran than Barry Hughes.

Martin   I did the flowers for your gran.

Nick   Sorry?

Martin   When she died . . . I remember sorting the
flowers out and that . . . for the funeral.

Nick   Yes. The flowers and that. Barry Hughes is an idiot.
If people only knew how bad some solicitors were.

Martin   Your Mary Duggan is one of his, isn't she?

Nick   What does Gary say about . . . your Barry?

Martin   Clients love him. Very loyal. Lot of loyalty.

Nick   You're not listening. What does Gary Mills say
about Barry Hughes?

Martin   How would I know?

Nick   Don't tell me, Martin . . . fuck off with the squeaky,
squeaky . . . don't tell me you haven't spent a beery
afternoon with Gary Mills . . . someone so promising . . . so
. . . talented. Just you and him. Gary not Barry. Cut out the
middle-man and pour lager down the real McCoy.

Martin   No. By the book.

Nick   Bollocks. What book?

Martin   I've got a wife and two saucepans. I can't afford to hang out with fuck-off heavies like Gary Mills.

Nick   You'd lie to anyone, wouldn't you?

Martin   Have it your way.

Nick   I will.

Martin   When Jake was born . . .

Nick   Yes?

Martin   It was . . .

Nick   Yes?

Martin   The first time I looked at him . . .

Nick   Were you there? For the birth?

Martin   Couldn't. I wouldn't have helped. Seeing Jane . . . you know . . . like that. Anyway. I looked at him and swore no one would hurt him. I'd kill anyone . . . don't tell Jane this, not ever . . . but I love that boy much more than her. I mean . . . it's different. It's blood, isn't it? It's the blood thing. He's my blood. Yeah? I love Jane, don't get me wrong . . . but she's not blood, is she? She had her life and I had my life and then we met . . . but Jake . . . you should have kids, you and Fran. Changes you. Blood.

Nick   Blood, right? Blood's the thing.

Martin   Yeah.

Nick   What's the game plan, Martin?

Martin   What?

Nick   What? Your subtlety takes my breath away.

Martin   What are you saying?

Nick   It's like watching Vinnie Jones trying to stroke a rabbit with the instep of his weaker foot.

Martin   I love it when you do that.

Nick   Don't change the subject.

Martin   No. No. When you're clever like that. The way you talk.

Nick   You were saying? And do me a favour – put in the high tackle now, cut the tiptoe shit.

Martin   Sorry?

Nick   What do you want to say to me, Martin?

Martin   All right. Family, isn't it? Bottom line. I mean . . . you know . . . I go off and that . . . you know . . . bit of whatever.

Nick   Whatever.

Martin   But at the end of the day . . .

Nick   In the cold light of morning . . .

Martin   Family counts, doesn't it?

Nick   At the end of the day.

Martin   Forget the rules and all that . . . forget the ethics shit . . . you know, the job side . . . bottom line is: family.

Nick   You should open a gift shop in Chancery Lane selling tea-towels with your homely homilies on: Family counts. Blood's the thing. Do you just forget, Martin? I mean, for example, have you just forgotten you're sleeping with a member of chambers? Do some facts just leave the room when you want them to?

Martin   We're talking about you.

Nick   Have you told Darling Campbell-Browne that she's a 'bit of whatever'. Do you whisper in her ear 'My bit of whatever'?

Martin   She knows the score. She's a grown-up.

Nick   By the way . . . did you vote Tory?

Martin   I'm not answering that.

Nick   So the answer is yes?

Martin   I'm not saying. Politics is private.

Nick   There you go – another tea-towel. 'Family counts.' 'Politics is private.' 'Forget the ethics shit.' You could be the next editor of the *Daily Mail*. Could you lend me some cash?

Martin   How much?

Nick   Hundred.

Martin *takes a large number of notes out of his back pocket and peels off two fifty-pound notes.*

Martin   Here.

Nick   Thanks. And get me some money in, can you? I mean, do some bloody work . . . at your desk in the clerks' room getting the money in work . . . not half the day in the pub with all your too many Spanish holiday-types work. I need some money.

Martin   For your elopement, right?

Nick   Big word for you.

Martin   Hundred enough?

Nick   Thanks.

Martin   Get you to Gretna.

A silence.

I don't vote Tory.

Nick   Right.

Martin   I fucking hate them.

Nick   Right.

Martin   Tell the truth I'm a bit insulted.

Nick   Right. More?

Nick *pours more champagne.*

Martin Bottom line?

Nick Another bottom line?

Martin Bottom, bottom line is: you're a cunt if you do this.

Nick So we're back to cunts.

Martin Yeah.

Nick Are you drunk?

Martin No.

Nick No. Of course not.

Martin You?

Nick Yes. Of course. Can I ask you something?

Martin Yeah.

Nick Can you sing 'Nessun Dorma'?

Martin No. I can't. Why?

Nick Nothing.

Martin My old dad could've. Sung it.

Nick Yes. Right.

Martin On the beach he . . .

Nick I know.

Martin Up and down the beach for twenty years. Opera. No crap. Only opera.

Nick I know.

Martin And he died . . .

Nick In a beach hut.

Martin By himself. No one should die by themselves.

Nick In Southend.

Martin   In a bloody beach hut. Mary Duggan. Deal with it. Manana, Nicky-boy.

Exit **Martin**.

Scene Three

Chambers. **Nick** *and* **Mary** *listening to the tape of her police interview.*

Policeman   This is your chance to give your side of the story, Mary. Mary? You don't live with anyone, do you?

Silence.

We know you don't live with anyone.

Silence.

So how did it get there?

Silence.

Mary?

Mary (*long pause*)   No comment.

Policeman   You can see our problem. It does look like it's yours, doesn't it? Mary? (*Pause.*) The drugs. How old are you, Mary?

Mary   One summer . . .

Policeman   Mary.

Mary   One summer, when I was fifteen . . .

Policeman   We've done this.

Mary   I ran away from home . . .

Policeman   Mary.

Mary   One summer . . .

Policeman   We're not listening to this again.

Nick *switches the tape off.*

Nick   I'm listening. I won't not listen. One summer . . .

Mary   One summer . . .

Nick   Go on.

Mary   I ran away from home. Not in the real sense . . . I spent the day . . . not at home . . . without telling them where I was.

Nick   Your parents.

Mary   You're listening.

Nick   Yes.

Mary   No. I mean . . . I know you're listening. You don't have to . . .

Nick   No.

Mary   Don't you think 'face the music' is a strange phrase? Wouldn't you say? My father had no music in him. Have you been up on the Downs? No. You should. For the sounds. There is space for each sound . . . each sound has its own time.

Nick   I can imagine.

Mary   Can you?

Nick   Yes.

Mary   I found a hole. It's called a witch hole. It's an old dew pond actually. It's a hidden place. All the walkers, all the cyclists, all the packed lunches go past. Above you. On top of the lip. Things . . . pass by. And you can't be seen. Under the lip. And so, that day, I was happy. The wind was soft, the grass was green and the end of the day was . . . elsewhere. And when I did go home . . . the long, dull punishment.
'We're disappointed in you, Mary.' We? My silent mother. Was she disappointed? She put down her knitting. Allying

herself to him with the putting down of her knitting.
Signalling her defeat. Her hands in her lap . . . her fingers
not moving . . . at all. And the ticking of the clock, the talk,
the talking to me, the telling me, the telling me.

'What are you without us, Mary?' Us?

My mother said nothing. Careful nothing in her eyes. The
ticking of the clock. The smell of bread. She made bread.
Do you know the smell? It slows down the air.

He made me take my clothes off and stand there in front of
them. 'That's what you are, Mary.'

And he sat and she sat and I stood. A planned, careful
shaming in steady time in slow air.

'Go to your room.' Finally. And some minutes later, a
decent interval, his brown slipper in the same slow time. I so
wanted to scream, not with the pain but with wanting to
break it up. I wanted to scream the house down. Six times,
of course six, in time-honoured fashion, well-spaced, his
breathing even – and it stayed even and with my face in the
pillow I pictured the dark hair in his nostrils and how it
moved when he breathed.

Nick   And then . . .

Mary   And then . . . he left and closed the door, in the
same way he had opened it, quietly and easily. How do you
close the door of a room in which you have beaten your
naked daughter? How do you close it quietly and easily and
with no . . . tenderness? That . . . blankness. How is it
possible, Mr Fernyhough?

Nick   I don't know.

Mary   I lay on the bed . . . I kept my face in the pillow . . .
and after a long time I heard the door open . . . and I knew
he was there again . . . standing . . . with his big hands at his
sides . . . just standing. Claiming the pain. Making it his.
Standing there. I got up from the bed and I didn't look at
the door, at him, I went to the window and looked out and
below on the grass there was a cat sleeping . . . the sun's
warmth . . . and I watched it and behind me my father

shifted his weight from one foot to the other and when the sun went the cat woke and stretched and washed and left and behind me he moved a little . . . and I didn't turn and I didn't turn and finally I felt him go. And I went downstairs and looked him in the eye.

Look I found this.

She takes a stone out of her pocket.

A witch's stone, do you think? I found it. He found me. My father. One day. In my hole. He found . . . my place. His hand came down from out of the blue . . . out of the blue . . . and pulled me out. I had the stone in my hand and I wanted to . . . I have it with me. I always have it with me. He held me here. By the shoulder. And pushed me home. All the way. I can feel it still.

Enter **Joe**.

Joe   Shit. Sorry.

Nick   Joe.

Joe   Sorry.

Nick   This is Mary Duggan.

Joe   Shit.

Mary   Hello.

Joe   I mean . . . hello. Not shit. I meant hello. Right. (*He starts to go.*) Wait. Do that again.

Mary   What?

Joe   Um . . . it might be very important.

Nick   Joe?

Joe   Would you mind taking your arms off the desk?

Mary   Oh. (*She does.*)

Joe Thank you. And then putting them back again . . . in your own time. Thank you. Excellent. Drink, Nick? When you've finished.

Nick Yeah.

Joe Good.

Exit **Joe**.

Mary Why did he . . .?

Nick He just liked your arms. He's honest. He says things.

Nick *switches the tape of the police interview back on.*

Mary My mother . . .

Policeman This has nothing to do with why we're here. Has it? Mary?

Mary She . . .

Policeman Mary.

Mary She never went out without it.

Policeman This is a waste of time. The drugs, Mary. Why were they there? One last chance, Mary.

Mary Mary, Mary.

Policeman So?

Mary (*long pause*) She put on a blue headscarf . . .

Policeman I'm terminating this interview. The time is ten forty-two and I'm switching the tape off now.

Nick *switches the tape off and looks at* **Mary**.

Mary She put on a blue headscarf whenever she went out. The same one. She never went out without it. It made her life outside the home into a series of errands. Silent, frightened tasks. There was a field next to the house. You couldn't cross it . . . you had to go round two sides of it . . .

the path was beneath the field . . . I mean, lower than the field. I used to see from the house . . . the headscarf sailing along the length of the field . . . just the blue headscarf. Sailing. Frightened. She lost it once. I came downstairs and saw her . . . all panicked, madness in her fingers . . . throwing her fingers all over the room . . . I found the scarf and she put it on and she took long enough putting it on – looking at me – to get the steadiness back. A blue headscarf. Like a clamp on her head.

Nick   We'll have the tape played. I want the jury to hear it.

Mary   But I don't say anything.

Nick   You're not allowed to say anything. Oppression. Fits the picture. The jury should hear it. It's better that way.

Mary   Don't.

Nick   What?

Mary   'It's better that way.' Don't.

Nick   Don't what?

Mary   What picture? Fits what picture?

Nick (*long pause*)   I'm going to get you out of this. Trust me.

Mary   I don't know.

Nick   Yes. Mary. Listen. Yes. Now. Look.
Eight police officers and a dog raid your flat. The numbers. Brighton police station hasn't got any money. So eight of them and a dog called Nero. Nine hairy bodies in your flat. It's not usual. And it helps us.

Mary   Does it?

Nick   First of all eight different policemen will never manage to say the same thing in the witness box. Second . . . the picture we can paint. Very large numbers of very large policemen with a great ugly dog on the one side and you on the other. Kick the door in. Hullabaloo to wake the dead . . .

and then . . . there's nothing there . . . just you, under the
duvet. What colour is your duvet?

Mary   White.

Nick   Good.

Mary   Good?

Nick   Excellent. Nightie?

Mary   What?

Nick   Colour?

Mary   It's a nightshirt.

Nick   Colour?

Mary   White.

Nick   Excellent. Peace and quiet. White and white.
Sleeping like an angel . . . you . . . like an angel.
Sledgehammer. Black boots. Out of the bloody blue. It's a
kind of rape. And no drugs. There has to be something to
show for it. I mean, they've woken up the neighbours.

Mary   I was . . .

Nick (*interrupting*)   Now. They enter the flat at 5.40 a.m.
The drugs are found at 6.20 a.m. Forty minutes. During
that time two disgruntled pigs pop out and bring something
back with them. Oh look. Oh my goodness. After forty
minutes searching this very small flat we've found a bag full
of heroin in the bread bin . . . next to the Mother's Pride.
Was it Mother's Pride? I shouldn't think so. Mary.

Mary   No.

Nick   Good. Hovis.

Mary   What? Maybe.

Nick   Good. Granary.

Mary   Good?

Nick   Granary. Mary.

Mary   Could have been.

Nick   Excellent.

Mary   Why?

Nick   Cobblestones. Sepia. Dvořák. Happy childhood.
Dirty knees. Happy England. Now. You've no idea how the
drugs got there – so it's one of two things – someone you
know put them there or our friends in blue did. Do you eat
toast?

Mary   What? Of course. Why?

Nick   How long before the police came had you last eaten
toast?

Mary   I don't know.

Nick   The evening before. Probably.

Mary   Maybe.

Nick   Probably the evening before. The Hovis. Granary
Hovis.

Mary   Possibly . . .

Nick   Yes. Anything else in the bread bin?

Mary   No.

Nick   Then it has to be police plant. You'd have seen the
heroin cuddling up to the Hovis, wouldn't you? In the
evening. When you had your toast. If it had been there.
What did you have on your toast?

Mary   I don't remember.

Nick   Shall we say honey? Could it have been honey?

Mary   It could have been.

Nick   Honey on granary. What kind of drug dealer is
that? And look . . . look at your hands, Mary Duggan. No

one, not even Joan of Arc, has such beautiful hands. Hands that get pricked? Long, cool arms shot up with fast poison? No. Not. Tiny veins. Thin, thin blood. Not those arms . . . Now. Sssh. Listen.

You were terrified. You've been woken up by eight men kicking your door down. You've got your nightshirt on. It's white. They have got big feet. Their teeth are yellow. Some of them have moustaches. They're practically Nazis. Snow White and the Nazis. Can you imagine, members of the jury, a bloody great moustache in your bedroom at 5.40 a.m. on a weekday morning – full of last night's fish and pickled onion? Can you imagine? Now. You couldn't see what they were doing all the time, could you? In your state of shock. Of course you couldn't. You are very scared. Are you going to notice if eight turns into six and back into eight again? Juries watch television. They know the shot. Girl under duvet . . . eyes and wrists peeking out. From under the duvet. Small wrists and big eyes. Versus old fish and onion and facial hair. Juxtapose.

Who's got the sweeter breath, members of the jury? Mary Duggan. That's who.

Mary I know all about the process. I know how the vulnerable get processed.

Nick Yes.

Mary Not them. Here. This.

Nick What?

Mary I know the sound.

Nick I'm not . . . Anyway. I have to. There is no choice.

Mary But it's not true. It won't be true. I could be anyone.

Nick Look – there isn't much time in there – you will go into the witness box and you will want to tell them everything about yourself . . . so they can judge you . . . you will leave the witness box feeling that you haven't said

enough and that no one has asked you the right questions. I
can't ask you about your father, I can't ask you about a
childhood in a hole. I have to give them what I can. I have
to get the essence of things across. Relevant essence.

Mary   A childhood in a hole? Is that all? There are things
that shouldn't run off the end of anyone's tongue. Essence?
What essence?

Nick   Mary Archer is fragrant. O. J. Simpson is black. It's
the lawyer's job to be shameless. I can't afford to have my
shame. You can't afford me to have any shame. Strong
brush strokes in a court of law, Mary. It's not about the
truth, the whole truth and nothing but the truth . . . there
just isn't time. It's not your fault and it isn't my fault. Of
course, it's up to you, I only do what you want me to do.

Mary   Are you good at it?

Nick (*long pause*)   Yes.

Mary (*long pause*)   Yes.

Nick   At the weekend . . . we're . . . I'm going to be in
Sussex. Firle. A place called Firle. A friend . . . someone in
chambers has a house. We'll be near each other. Funny.
Funny.

Mary   Funny.

Nick   I thought we could . . .

Mary   Yes.

Nick   I mean . . . not like this.

Mary   No.

Nick   Somewhere . . . proper. Would that be . . . would it?

Mary   I was early today. I got here early. So I went to a
café.

Nick   Where?

Mary   A café on the Gray's Inn Road.

Nick Right.

Mary Why?

Nick I was just . . .

Mary What?

Nick Picturing it. All faded and yellow and steamy and warm.

Mary If you like. A man came in.

Nick Did he?

Mary Yes.

Nick I mean . . . yes, sorry . . . a man came in . . .

Mary He was bow-legged like an old horse . . . and he sat by himself and asked for mince and potatoes and cabbage. And my heart went out to him. I told myself the story of his life that had brought him to mince and potatoes and cabbage at half past four on the Gray's Inn Road. He had tea with his food. Four sugars . . . administered. And he ate without looking up. He was still there when it was time for me to come here and I left the café and crossed the road and I looked back and I could see the back of his head and the back of his head made me want to cry. His poor head. And then a whole group of men and women went through the door of the café, all of a bustle . . . and they went to the table where the sad man sat and hello'd and hello'd and slapped him on the back and ruffled his hair and together they filled up the whole place with their limbs stretched and their big talk. And there was no sadness. And I came here feeling foolish and lonely. Very lonely.

Nick Can I kiss you, Mary Duggan?

Mary Other people's sadness. It's easy to fall in love with other people's sadness.

Nick Mary . . .

Mary   He knows . . . my father . . . about the case . . . my arrest . . . the trial. And he'll come and find me. Before Monday. It's what he does. He sniffs out . . . my moments. He pours himself into them . . . my bad moments . . . his self-pity, his sentiment, Mary, Mary, Daddy, Daddy. He hit me and hit me all through my childhood and you'd think . . . now . . . that all the pain was his. He's stealing my pain.

Nick   Don't look at him.

Mary   What?

Nick   Look. Outside. On the lawn.

Mary   Where?

Nick   Wherever you like.

Mary   Saturday. Sunday. Before Monday. The witches' hole.

Nick   The dew pond.

Mary   Are you going to kiss me?

Nick   Yes. Mary Duggan.

They kiss. A knock at the door. Enter **Martin**.

Martin   Solicitor's here, sir.

Nick   He's late.

Martin   I'll get him.

Nick   What's the point of turning up an hour late?

Martin   I'll get him.

Nick   We've finished. Actually.

Martin   Right. I'll show you out, Miss.

Mary   It's all right. I know the way.

Exit **Mary**.

Nick   Is Darling still in chambers?

Martin   Yeah.

Nick   I thought I might . . .

Martin   What?

Nick   Firle. At the weekend. You wouldn't mind?

Martin   No. Good con?

Nick   What do you care?

Martin   Oh, I care. How is the Doris shaping up?

Nick   She's . . .

Martin   What?

Nick   Sad.

Martin   Yeah? Why's that then?

Nick   She's going to be in a hole up on the South Downs. At the weekend.

Martin   The South Downs.

Nick   It's a witches' hole?

Martin   Oh yeah?

Nick   She used to go there a lot . . .

Martin   Did she?

Nick   And now . . . it doesn't matter. Shall I check with Darling? About the weekend.

Martin   Yeah. Check. Joe could come. Maybe.

Nick   Yeah. Maybe. She's got this stone. She carries it around all of the time. In her pocket. A witches' stone. Sorry. Forget it. I'm . . . I'm off. Night, Martin.

Exit **Nick**.

Martin   Night, sir. (*Lovingly.*) Cunt. Stupid cunt.

Scene Four

Nick *and* **Fran**'s *bathroom*.

Fran   You've been home for two hours.

Nick   Yes.

Fran   And it takes you two hours to mention this . . . plan.

Nick   What do you mean?

Fran   It's Thursday night. Darling Campbell-Browne has asked – us? – to go down to Sussex for the weekend. Simple question. Why did you wait two hours before mentioning it? Tell me about the process.

Nick   This is ridiculous.

Fran   Do you want me to come?

Nick   Of course.

Fran   Your voice goes up an octave.

Nick   What?

Fran   When you . . .

Nick   When I . . . Go on. When I . . . What?

Fran   Do you want me to come?

Nick   I want you to come.

Fran   And then with superhuman effort you bring it back down again and do the best you can with your eyes.

Nick   Fran.

Fran   Steady gaze, Nick. Very good. But I've seen your eyes look at me . . . I've seen how they *can* look at me . . . remember? Do actually try to remember.

Nick   When you're in this kind of mood . . .

Fran   Don't.

Nick   It's . . . terrible.

Fran   It's not my mood.

Nick   Yes, it is.

Fran   It is not my mood. It's your mood. That's the whole point. Why can't you just be honest. You don't want me to come to Darling's. Do you? Why?

Nick   I didn't say I didn't.

Fran   But you don't. Tell the truth. It would be so much easier.

Nick   It's just . . .

Fran   Yes?

Nick   You'd be determined to have a bad time.

Fran   Thanks. Thanks a lot.

Nick   Wouldn't you?

Fran   Thank you very much, Nick.

Nick   Oh, fine. Is that it? Are you satisfied? Are we at the bottom now? You keep fucking asking . . . you keep asking . . . jabbing away . . . and then I tell you and you get all . . . Jesus. You asked, Fran.

Nick   Maybe I've got it all wrong. Maybe there is no process to tell me about. Maybe I'm so far away it takes two hours to get round to a thing like this nowadays.

Nick   Fran, look at me. I want you to come.

Fran   The words well-spaced, the sentence complete.

Nick   Well?

Fran   I remember when your eyes . . .

Nick   No. Stop. I want you to come. End of story. Stop all this. I just want you to come . . . all right? You need a break. Sleep and eat . . . all that.

Fran   All right, Nick.

Nick   All right. We can watch Martin and Darling do their thing.

Fran   Yes.

Nick   The death of hope. Cynicism, greed, opportunism, lust . . . all in a kind of sick contract.

Fran   Have we finished?

Nick   What?

Fran   Our talk.

Nick   It's like they have an agreement. Eyes open; tits out; willy and wonga; dosh and donga. Terrifying really.

Fran   We're lucky.

Nick   Terrifying.

Fran   Aren't we, Nick?

Nick   Yeah.

Fran   I'm sorry. I'm sorry, Nick.

Nick   It's all right.

Fran   It's just . . . I miss you.

Nick   Then you better come to Sussex.

Fran   Will you promise me something?

Nick   Anything.

Fran   Something. Talk to me as much as you talk to them.

Nick   God, Fran.

Fran   You know what I mean. Don't go off. Don't get on a different bus.

Nick   A different bus?

Fran   A different bus. Did I say that?

Nick You said that.

Fran That's the stupidest . . .

Nick It's the stupidest thing you've ever said, doctor.

Fran Sorry.

Nick That's all right.

Fran I love you.

Nick 'Baby I Love You'. The Ronettes or The Ramones?

Fran It's not that easy, Nick.

Nick No.

Fran Charm isn't enough.

Nick No.

Fran The Ronettes.

Nick Why?

Fran They took themselves seriously. The Ramones were self-conscious. They knew how they looked. Camp isn't camp when it calls itself camp.

Nick You're right. You're always right.

Fran Cuddle.

Nick Cuddle.

They cuddle.

I've got a bit of work to do.

Fran It's late.

Nick Is it?

Fran Yes. I'll be asleep.

Nick OK.

Fran Night.

Nick Night.

Fran Nick . . .

Nick I love you too.

Fran Nabokov collected butterflies.

Nick Did he?

Fran Yes.

Nick I should . . .

Fran Work.

Nick Yes.

Fran Not a complete hag.

Nick No.

Fran Poor Mary Duggan.

Nick Yeah.

Act Two

Scene One

The kitchen of **Darling**'s *house in Sussex.*

Darling   For what we are about to receive . . . (*She crosses herself.*)

Nick   You're the worst Catholic I've ever seen.

Darling   Thank you, Nicholas.

Nick   You even cross yourself the wrong way round.

Joe   How do you know?

Nick   Maradona. Hand of God.

Joe   Maradona. Crossing himself the right way round with the hand of God.

Fran   The Pope was a goalkeeper . . . apparently.

Joe   I wish I was married to you, Fran.

Nick   Anyway, you're a terrible Catholic.

Darling   My Catholicism is a battle.

Joe   As in sleeping with our senior clerk and talking to God at the same time.

Darling   As I said . . . it's a battle, darling. And sleeping with a married man is a sin all by itself. There's nothing about senior clerks. It's not more sinful because it's a senior clerk. It's the sleeping and the marriage, Joseph.

Fran   Where is he?

Joe   Martin? Pub. The Ram.

Fran   Of course.

Darling   As I was saying . . .

Nick   What were you saying?

Darling   Grace, darling. Grace. For what we are about to receive may the Lord make us truly thankful.

Nick   Amen.

Joe   Amen.

Nick   Amen. Do you remember? The sleeping Judge Richards.

Fran   Jesus.

Nick   Not just dozing.

Joe   No.

Nick   Not just post-lunch sleepiness.

Joe   No.

Nick   Totally gone.

Joe   In the middle of your speech.

Fran   Who is this *for*?

Nick   And then he woke up. Suddenly. And when he woke he didn't have a clue.

Joe   Had he been asleep? How long for? Where was he?

Nick   And it just came out . . . in the moment between sleeping and walking and before thought. An involuntary thing. His most honest sound.

Joe   Amen, he said. Amen. His knee-jerk jerked-awake word was Amen.

Fran   The first death I had . . . my first patient to die . . . she died suddenly . . . I spent a lot of time with her after she died. I wanted to . . . do it properly. I don't know. And when the family came, the son I think it was, said a prayer . . . at the bedside with them all gathered round in their coats. Amen, they said. Perfectly together. Amen all at the same time.

Nick   You've never told me that.

Fran   No. It's nobody's business.

Nick   Until now.

Darling   He touched my backside once – Judge Richards. In a friendly sort of way. I was drinking sherry. He touched my backside. His palm, I think. The whole of his palm on the backside.

Nick   I hate that. I hate it when barristers knock judges.

Joe   Yes. Back off, Darling. Back off with your backside.

Nick   Probably you backed into his palm.

Joe   Like a red Ferrari nudging the bumper of a very lovely old green Bentley.

Fran   Did you know that Nabokov was a lepidopterist? By the way. While we're waiting . . .

Nick   Waiting?

Joe   Really? Amazing.

Fran   Amazing.

Nick   Fran.

Fran   He discovered new species. *Madeleina lolita.*

Joe   What? Really?

Fran   *Pseudolucia humbert.*

Joe   No.

Fran   Yes. Actually.

Joe   Brilliant.

Fran   Amazing. They're Latin-American blues. *Lolita* and *humbert.* How long do you suppose they'd been around without a name? Before him. Before Nabokov found them. With his net and his white cotton gloves.

Joe   White cotton gloves.

Fran   It's what he wore. For butterfly hunting. Delicate hands, you see. Cotton gloves out there in the heat of the day.

Nick   Waiting for what, Fran?

Fran   Sometimes I see you go past . . . your legs are moving, your mouth is opening and closing . . . but you're thirty feet up in the air . . . moving and talking thirty feet up . . . and you skip and spin and laugh . . . but you have no weight. I've stopped trying to pull you down. I just wait. For you to get off the fucking bus.

Nick *looks at* **Joe**.

Fran   Don't.

Nick   Fran . . .

Fran   If you look at him . . . if you dare to look at him . . .

Darling   The soup is cold.

Joe   Shame.

Darling   I mean, it's cold.

Joe   Yeah.

Darling   No.

Joe   No?

Darling   It's meant to be cold.

Joe   Oh.

Darling   Fortunately. Given the noise we're all making. The time we're having. Gazpacho. Cold soup.

Joe   That's . . . good.

Darling   Exactly. It's a question of reassurance. There is no rush. The soup can wait. I'm sure none of you will think me rude if I make a start, though.

Fran   I don't know how you do it.

Darling   One day, Frances, you and I should have a talk
. . . without these boys. We'll slip off, shall we? Make sure
they have all they need, a cosy enough den . . . and then
we'll slip away for a bit of a talk. I'd like that.

Fran (*pause*)   I'd like that too.

Darling   Try the soup . . . if you're ready . . . no
particular hurry, but . . . one should eat before it gets to
room temperature.

Enter **Martin**.

Martin   Hello.

Darling   I think in our collective unconscious we've all
been waiting for you. We sat down some time ago and no
one has started. You missed grace but you're in time for the
soup.

Martin   Cheers. (*He sits and tries the soup.*) It's cold.

Darling   I'll heat it up for you.

Exit **Darling** *with* **Martin**'s *bowl.*

Martin (*to everyone*)   All right? No one fancy the soup
then?

His mobile phone rings. He takes it out of his pocket.

Yeah.

He listens for some time and then stands up, still on the phone.

Joe-boy. Tell her, will ya. Gimme ten minutes.

Exit **Martin** *still on the phone, listening.*

Enter **Darling**, *with soup bowl.*

Joe   He said, 'Joe-boy. Tell her, will ya. Gimme ten
minutes.'

Darling   My pour soup. The things a girl will do for a bit of rough. Shall we start again? For what we are about to receive may the Lord make us truly thankful.

Joe   I did a trial last year . . .

Nick   A trial. Well done.

Joe   Shut up, Nick.

Darling   Yes, Nicholas, all this chipping in . . .

Joe   Piece of crap at Southwark. Client held a knife to a boy's throat in a phone box in Soho.

Fran   Boy?

Joe   Boy. Twenty-something.

Fran   Boy?

Joe   Boy. Man. Whatever.

Fran   Whatever.

Joe   Anyway. Victim was gay.

Fran   *The* victim.

Joe   Sorry?

Fran   Not 'victim was gay', *the* victim was gay. It's tiresome – shorthand of that kind and something tells me it's not how you'd like to sound. Weary and cynical won't be the point, will it? Of what we are about to receive. That would be to misunderstand your . . .

Joe   My what?

Fran   Oh, you know, Joe – your agony, your war within – the spin-dryer that is your lawyer soul.

Nick   All this chipping in.

Darling   Go on, Joseph, I'm rapt.

Joe   The victim was gay. The defence was he asked me for sex.

Nick   Like you do.

Joe   I said yes. He gave me forty quid up front and I ran off with it. Sort of opportunist con.

Nick   Form?

Fran   Form?

Joe   Lots, actually. Pages and pages. Plenty of knifepoint robbery . . . even one in a phone box in Soho a couple of years before. Anyway, we had to establish that the victim was gay – I wasn't going to call my thick-as-shit-jumpy-as-hell-robber client and in the witness box the victim wasn't queenie at all. I mean, your average Southwark jury wouldn't have seen it. I'd have put my case to him and the jury would have said, hang on . . .

Nick   Hang on there . . .

Joe   He's no John Inman. He's no Danny La Rue, therefore he's not . . .

Nick   A ho-mo-sex-ual.

Joe   Therefore my bloke must be guilty. So I had to ask. Are you gay or are you straight? I thought I'd make sure he knew I wasn't . . . I said 'gay', I said 'straight'. I thought the words . . . I thought I'd tell him.

Darling   Yes, darling?

Joe   That I wasn't homophobic. I thought 'gay', 'straight' would tell him that. The words. Don't you find you're always compensating for the silly clothes? I mean . . . on the face of it . . . people with horsehair on their heads don't look like *Guardian* readers. The judge said: 'Homosexual and heterosexual in my court, please.' I could have kissed him. He made me repeat it. I pretended not to have heard. 'I'm sorry, your honour?' 'Homosexual or heterosexual.' I looked at the boy. That told him. It was as good as a wink.

Nick   Or a nod.

Joe   Or a nod.

Fran   Well, thank God. Well done, Joe Page, conscience intacta.

Joe   To his credit the boy said: 'Why should I answer that?' I looked at the judge. 'I'm asking you for a very good reason,' I said, putting plenty of I'm-only-doing-my-job-this-hurts-me-too in my voice – still looking at the judge. He had no choice, despite himself, the man with the most horsehair on his head. 'You'll have to answer the question,' he said. 'Both,' said my victim. Pin-drop. 'I'm bisexual.' Pin-drop. And I knew from the silence that it was all over. I knew the jury would turn to prejudice. And all of them, each one, about two seconds into the silence, moved in their seats. If prejudice were a gesture it would be the shifting of buttocks. I took a long time to ask the next question. The victim started to look around from the witness box so long was the next question in coming. No one else was looking around. They were looking at the ground. 'Yes, Mr Page?' the judge said. He thought I was milking the moment. He was a brilliant witness, that boy, never put a foot wrong. Obviously honest. Overwhelming case, embarrassing really – on paper. My client was acquitted in fourteen minutes. Not guilty. 'A verdict beyond your wildest dreams, Mr Page,' the judge said, before the jury foreman had even sat down. Why did I ask the question? I had an honest reason . . . I had a proper professional purpose . . . but I knew what it might mean . . . and I asked it.

Darling   Of course you asked it, darling.

Joe   My client left the dock punching the air and saying: Yes. Yes. Over and over. Yes. Yes.

Darling   The innocent ones collapse in a heap.

Joe   And the guilty ones punch the air.

Darling   Always the same . . . poor old *air* . . . getting punched all the time.

Joe He shook my hand . . . outside, later . . . you know, good strong handshake, man to man. And I said: Well done. Well done, for fuck's sake. Well done?

Fran You've told that story more than once.

Joe Sorry.

Fran I wonder why.

Nick Fran.

Fran No platforms here, Nicholas. Audience participation, I'm afraid. People listening to it for the first time – I remember, actually – stops them in their tracks all right, moves them, Joe, but part of it, of course, is that you're delighted that you got him off. Against the odds. It's perfect. He got off *and* you're left with a conscience struggle *and* it's a struggle you can share with others at dinner parties *and* dinner parties will love you for it. And actually, Joe, you're fine, aren't you? I mean, that's where you're at and that's where you're content to stay – doing your job, spending your money and weeping through your teeth in front of your friends every now and again. And quiet hands will touch your arm and press your shoulder. It's a funny way to live, Joe – in constant pursuit of reassurance.

Darling I win cases because I've got gorgeous tits. As soon as they start to sag, you watch, my win curve will go down with them. Lovely big upwardly mobile tits. That's my secret.

Nick Not a secret . . . really. Darling.

Joe I'm going for a piss.

Darling Good luck, Joseph. Thank you for telling us.

Exit **Joe**.

Fran Do you think he'll manage all by himself?

Darling Never laugh at a man when he's showing you his wounds. It's the best they can manage, that's all. One can't

expect more. Here's my wound. Love me. That's not so
bad.

Nick Hello.

Darling Sorry, Nicholas. Feeling a bit left out? You know
how we women do talk . . . and sometimes we quite forget
you're there. Wonderful wine.

Enter **Joe**.

Here's to my tits. Everyone. To my fabulous tits.

Nick/Joe To Darling's tits.

Enter **Martin**.

Martin You keep off her tits.

Darling That's my boy.

Martin I love 'em.

Darling Bless you.

Martin I mean, I really love 'em.

Darling Darling.

Martin *sits down and looks at bowl of soup.*

He looks at **Darling**.

Martin Fuck it. I'll have it cold. I don't care.

Darling For what he's about to receive may the Lord
make him truly thankful.

Martin Cheers. (*Tries soup.*) It's all right – cold.

Darling You're *so* gorgeous.

Scene Two

In the kitchen. **Darling** *is preparing to cook a chicken.*

Darling   Where are the boys?

Fran   Having a talk while us girls make the Sunday lunch. In the gazebo probably, plotting a murder.

Darling   Not the gazebo. They're very important men. Important men like to walk when they're being important. You can say dangerous things when you're walking. The gazebo is too Julie Andrews for men of their importance.

Fran   Not really Sicily.

Darling   No. Much too Sussex. No one has ever been gunned down at Glyndebourne.

Joe   Us girls? I'm honoured. I've dreamed of being a girl. Actually I've dreamed of being a girl backing vocalist. A Supreme – ideally. I'd love to have been a Supreme. They're in the gazebo. Smoking. It's the closest they can get to a bike shed. Probably they'll swear a bit and spit and stuff.

Darling   You'd have made a lovely Supreme, darling.

Joe   Thank you.

Fran   Have you been to Sicily, Joe?

Joe   Yes. And Glasgow.

Darling   Watch. This is clever. This is very clever. Half fill the empty beer can with white wine. *Comme ça.* Watch, darlings.

Joe   I gave blood once in Glasgow. I mean voluntarily. Here's some blood. Here's a cup of tea. I was twenty-two.

Fran   You remember how old you were?

Darling   And then . . . under the skin with your hands . . . (*She puts hands under the skin of the chicken.*) And that's where the

butter and the garlic goes. I do love a bit of rural cooking –
hands on, hands in, up to the elbow cooking.

Joe   The nurse taking my blood . . .

Darling   Was she gorgeous? One of those Glasgow
lovelies.

Joe   Yes. She was. And she asked me what I did. I'd just
started pupillage. So I told her. I'm a barrister, I said. And I
told her how uncomfortable I was with all the pomp and
circumstance at the bar. And she said . . .

Darling   What did she say?

Joe   She said: 'You're the same.' 'No, I'm not,' I said. She
didn't say anything more. Her eyes were filled with . . .
conviction.

Darling   And then she took your blood. Fabulous.

Fran   Is that as seminal as your seminal moments get, Joe?
Fifteen years ago you spent three minutes with someone
who didn't buy your line in disaffection and you're still not
over it?

Joe   I'm going upstairs.

Fran   That's called walking away.

Joe   Yes. It is.

Fran   The story has a point. You're obviously desperate to
discuss your . . . whatever it is . . .

Joe   See you later.

Fran   Why not with me? Joe. Why not with me?

Joe   Because you sound a touch personal, Fran. Why don't
you argue with Nick instead.

Fran   Why? Why did you say that?

Joe   I'm not his bodyguard. You don't have to beat the
shit out of me to get to him.

Fran   What has he said to you?

Joe   Nothing.

Fran   No. Not nothing. Clearly . . . not nothing.

Darling   And finally . . . a parting of the buttocks and on she goes.

She places the chicken on to the beer can so that most of the beer can is inside the chicken.

See you later, Joe.

Exit **Joe**.

Fran   I can't believe you did that.

Darling (*pause*)   I did a lot of family work when I was at the bar. It's a clerks' room equation – women do family law and rape. Men do crime.

Fran   Why are you telling me this?

Darling   I was sent along to Marylebone Magistrates Court one morning to represent a mother whose daughter had been placed with foster parents. The brief, which I'd been handed at ten to seven the night before, told me that the foster parents had been using my client's thirteen-year-old daughter as a prostitute and that her pubic hair, which had just started to grow, making her older than her . . . clients required, had been shaved off with a disposable razor one Saturday night by the foster father who was very drunk at the time and he'd cut her badly and now she was in hospital. Would I be so good, said my brief, to inform the mother, my client, all about these charming goings-on? That's what the brief said – 'These charming goings-on.' I got to court. The mother was a Muslim. Devout as devout can be. She spoke no English. We had never met before, of course. There was an interpreter – male – who arrived an hour late. He had eczema all over his face and hands. I sat on a wooden bench with my male interpreter scratching himself on one side and my client on the other side and I explained to her through him all about the slicing up of her daughter's vagina. My

client's face was covered. I could only see her eyes. I've
never seen such . . . defeat. And I got it wrong. I mean, in
myself. I wanted to be sad but I was only angry. I fought like
hell to get the child back with the mother. My God I fought.
Look what the local authority have done for her – sliced
vagina for God's sake. I kicked and screamed and shouted
and no one was watching or listening. After it was all over
and it had gone against me, I went into Regent's Park and
sat on a bench and then I went to the zoo and watched two
gibbons fucking and screaming like car alarms and . . . I
made the decision. To stay at the bar. I got the agony over
with once and for all, darling. But I do understand . . . the
line in disaffection . . . Joe . . . leave him alone, darling.

Fran   It's not me. It's them. They bring these things up
. . . they bring themselves up and then . . . they don't . . .
they won't take it seriously. They won't work hard. I don't
know. I'm not sure what I'm saying. I'm sick of playing hide
and seek. I just want to talk.

Darling   You can't shout all the time. A lighter touch is
better. Let them run around the way they do.

Fran   Sleep with them if needs be. I'm sorry. I didn't
mean to . . . that came out wrong.

Darling   I don't see how it could have come out . . . not
wrong.

Fran   Sorry.

Darling   There's no need to apologise.

Fran   You process the sliced vaginas. And I patch them
up. Stitch. Patch. Back you go. The two of us, Darling.

Darling   We have things in common. I wonder why we
sound so different?

Fran   You've given up.

Darling   Shrillness doesn't suit me. Sorry. Sorry.

Fran   I don't have . . . anyone to talk to. I've been getting it all wrong. People are much worse than . . . I'm sorry. I don't feel very . . . solid. Where is he?

Darling   Nick.

Fran   Where does he go? I can't find him any more.

Enter **Martin** *and* **Nick**.

Martin   That chicken's got a can of Four X up its arse.

Darling   Well, bugger me.

Scene Three

Outside.

Martin   I love it.

Nick   What?

Martin   Sunday lunch. I fucking love it.

Nick   She's a good cook.

Martin   She's a brilliant cook.

Nick   Yes.

Martin   She's a fucking chef. Tell you something else. She's got a great duvet. Just white. That's it. It's just white. No fucking about. No swirls or fucking patterns. White. Class. Sets her off nice. Background. Like in a photo booth. Except it's white and not that fucking manky old orange colour. She says Fran knows.

Nick   She's wrong.

Martin   Nah. She's right. Women know about other women. I've got a lot of respect for Fran.

Nick   Have you?

Martin   Yeah. What you doing, sir? I know what sort of
head you've got on. It's why I've won every time I've went
to Vegas.

Nick   What are you talking about? Vegas?

Martin   You've got to go with a silly head. Serious head,
all Uh. Uh. Uh. and you're fucked. Gotta be a silly head.
Right. Bink. There's a grand. Oh. Lucky me. There's two
grand. Oh. Lucky me again. Bink. There's four grand. Oh
so lucky. Oh so fucking lucky. Good night. God bless. And
thank you. Walking on water. I think so. You've got a silly
head on. You can't lose. Bink. Bink. Bink. Crazy, silly head.
But. But it's always gonna change into a serious head in the
end – you watch. Then you'll lose it. Believe me. Uh. Uh.
Uh. Goodbye.

Nick   You're a very weird man.

Martin   Maybe. You didn't answer my question. What
are you going to do?

Nick   I don't know.

Martin   Well, someone's gotta know. Soon. Haven't they?
Nicky-boy? It's not too late. Just forget you ever met her.
Fran's not stupid . . . she'll be all right.

Nick   You can't clerk my life, Martin.

Martin   You don't get it, do you? I can smell stink a mile
off. It's my job. And this case . . . this whole thing is a stinker.
It's covered in wet shit. Don't you see? She's got you just
where she wants you . . . you're her insurance policy. If this
doesn't go right for her . . . you know what she'll do, don't
you? It won't be thanks very much, Mr F, see you in five
years' time when I get out of Holloway. Will it? Sir?

Nick   Not everyone's like you, Martin.

Martin   Oh yes they are. Everyone's like me. Ask Fran.
What do you think the Court of Appeal would make of her

brief doing what you've been doing? I'm telling you. Bottom line. Mary Duggan. There's a skunk in her cunt.

Nick   Jesus. Jesus. You're an animal. A complete animal.

Martin   Yeah. Well. Don't start crying about it, Nicky-boy. You lot . . . I mean, I love you all . . . I do. I love you. I . . . care about you . . . but you can't, can you? You all go back to . . . what is it? You can't hack it, can you? The really hard stuff. You're all a bit soft in the middle. Aren't you? Hand on heart. You need me . . . every time you need me. You lot. The end of the day you're all little boys. Don't get me wrong – I love you.

Nick   You worry me. You really worry me.

Martin   And you worry me. And I love you. So . . . I look after you. You weren't thinking of taking a walk, I hope?

Nick   What?

Martin   You won't be going for a walk up on the Downs all on your tod, will ya? Looking for witches with skunky old cunts. Sir?

Nick   You make me sick.

Martin   As I said – someone's gotta know. Soon.

Nick   I'll make my mind up.

Martin   Maybe.

Nick   I'm going for a walk.

Martin   Are you?

Nick   Yes. You?

Martin   The Ram.

Nick   With me? Martin?

Martin *neither indicates assent nor dissent.*

Exit **Nick**.

Scene Four

The kitchen. **Fran** *alone. Enter* **Joe**.

Joe   Fran.

Fran   Joe.

Joe   They're all mad . . . here . . . they're mad.

Fran   Good walk?

Joe   There were people . . .

Fran   Were there?

Joe   A family taking their llamas for a walk.

Fran   Llamas.

Joe   Like you do. On a Sunday afternoon. Two fucking
llamas on leads . . . dum-di-dum down the village street.
'Good afternoon.' 'Good afternoon. Lovely weather.'
You've got two fucking llamas on leads. Look. What do you
mean 'Good afternoon. Lovely weather?' What about the
llamas? And then, at the post office there was a Chinese
woman up a ladder . . . she was twenty-something . . . and
an older white man holding the ladder at the bottom. She
was using a trowel to clear the gutter . . . and she dropped it
– the trowel. 'Sorry, Dad,' she said. 'Nearly hit me, Mum,'
he said. Mum. Mum? Not a child in sight. Completely mad.
What are they talking about? Mum? Dad?

Fran   Mum. Dad.

Joe   Yes.

Fran   What are they talking about?

Joe   And then . . . a cricket match on the village green –
hundreds of vicars and a blacksmith with Agincourt
forearms on each team and fleets of bicycles with baskets on
the front . . . very lovely, very . . . you know . . .

Fran   Yes. Very.

Joe   And at tea in the cricket – the other village all out for a hundred and twenty-eight – the old woman and her middle-aged son who were sitting near me on the boundary – in chairs, in front of their car – got out their own tea . . . they had knives and spoons and white crockery and heavy white napkins and the mother stirred and spread and they ate and sipped and dabbed at their wet and crumby lips with the heavy white napkins and after their tea the son got out yesterday's *Daily Mail* and passed part of it to his mother without a word and I thought this isn't lovely . . . actually . . . at all.

Fran   Good walk, then?

Joe   Yes. No. Jesus, Fran.

Fran   I'm sorry?

Joe   'Good walk, then?' What's that? I'm telling you about seeing two llamas out for a walk on a Sunday afternoon in Firle village.

Fran   No, you're not.

Joe   Do you think I should *not* have told you? Should I just not have told you?

Fran   And poor old Joe likes it in Firle, he's seduced by Sunday afternoon and then he remembers he used to live in Brixton when he was a student and he had a miner to stay, his very own miner (does he take sugar?), and Joe thinks . . . maybe Firle isn't so wonderful. There we are. There we are. At the moment – the sound of you – I couldn't give a fuck. Frankly.

Joe   This is you. This is all you. You're the angry one. I don't know why . . .

Fran   Don't you? You tell me, Joe, what you think I'm angry about. No. You won't. Of course not. Do you know what I like about my job? Pain. People in pain. People in bed, howling. And I make them sleep. And we're honest . . . both of us. It's what I want . . . now . . . it's what is left.

Joe   Fran . . .

Fran   Yes?

Joe   Nothing.

Fran   You might have been a decent man, Joe. Instead . . .
you're a liar. What were you going to say, Joe?

Joe   Nothing.

Enter **Martin** *and* **Nick**.

Martin   We saw two fucking llamas. Thanks very much.
How's your fucking father? Out for a stroll.

Nick   Amazing.

Fran   On leads.

Nick   What?

Fran   What?

Nick   On leads.

Martin   Yeah. Brilliant. Leads. I'm gonna live here. What
do you reckon? Hour and a half door to door on a Monday
morning? I'm gonna live here and buy *ten* llamas. Been to
church, Mr Page? I think not. I had a word with the vicar
. . . they missed you . . . don't you worry, I said, fucking
Songs of Praise – I'll make sure he watches *Songs of Praise*.
Where's Darling?

Fran   Out.

Martin   I saw you, Joe, having a look . . . having a gander
up the skirt of that Chinese bird on the ladder. Dropped her
spade, she did, she was so overcome. Chinese. Bit unusual in
a place like this.

Fran   Did you see her, Nick? The Chinese bird.

Nick   Yeah.

Fran   What did she say?

Nick   What? Nothing. I don't think she said anything. Just . . . dropped her spade.

Fran   Spade.

Nick   Fran.

Fran   Big spade?

Nick   Yes.

Martin   Do you know what they call it? When the dogs are chasing a fox – and they do all that howling – they call it 'giving tongue'. Brilliant. I'm gonna live here. *Songs of Praise* for you, I think, Mr Page? Where did you say she was?

Fran   I didn't.

Martin   Giving tongue. Brilliant.

Joe   Brilliant.

Fran   You know, don't you? My God. You all know. Of course. I'm the last. Of course. Thank you, Nicholas . . . thank you for . . . tell your . . . tell these . . . people . . . tell your bloody clerk . . . of course. You're covering for him, aren't you? Martin? Aren't you? Was he fucking another woman and pretending to be with you? Look . . . um . . . I think I'm . . . I'm going to . . . you fucking bastard. You fucking bastard.

She starts to hit **Nick** *who does little to protect himself.*

You . . . fucking . . . bastard. It's her, isn't it? Your stupid bloody client. Mary Duggan. Mary Duggan. Mary Duggan.

Martin *grabs hold of* **Fran**.

Fran   Get off me. Get off me. Oh my God. Oh my God.

Fran *stops struggling.* **Martin** *still holds her.*

Enter **Darling**.

Darling   The evening is heavenly, darlings. Let go of her, Martin. There's something about dusk. Here. Heavenly.

She gets a drink and gives it to **Fran**.

Have a drink, Frances. Here's the news:
Firle were all out for a hundred and twenty-two. Six runs
short Mrs Vicar told me. Six runs short. What might have
been. If only. Still. Sit down, darling. Drink the drink. And
Mrs Manor with her basket of vegetables . . . on her arm,
the way it should be . . . marrow and carrots, I think. Sit
down, darling. (**Fran** *does*.) And Mrs Widow watering her
peonies with a very small watering-can (as befits her
widowhood) and all the care and concern of the village with
her as she waters. And I wonder, don't you, what can go
wrong? And past the blue doors of the Alms houses and
'Land of Hope and Glory' from a sitting-room window and,
of course, it's the Last Night of the Proms. And what can go
wrong? With anything. The walk home . . . But close the
door . . . close the door and here we are . . . here we all are
screaming and shouting and pulling and pushing. Such a
noise.

Fran   You know too. Don't you? Of all . . . of all . . .
you're such a liar. How could you . . .

Darling   I shall make us some supper. Something simple.
Nicholas . . . I'll show you all I know about omelette
cooking.

Fran   What?

Darling   The rest of you . . . leave us alone.

Fran   What?

Darling   Out you go, darlings. One by one, I think. Walk
in different directions.

Fran   Who do you think you are? You can't . . .

Darling   Martin . . . the pub. Bring me back six different
beer mats. Joe . . . the cricket pitch . . . six four-leafed
clovers.

Fran   You're mad. You're all mad. What are you talking about?

Darling   Fran . . . Firle House – the grounds. Count the cows, darling. They've got numbers pinned to their ears. Number forty-seven is a very beautiful cow. Find her, Fran. Look into her eyes. We'll be an hour. Omelettes in an hour. Off you go.

Fran   You can't . . . this is all mad. Nick? Say something. Please. For once . . . now . . . say *something*.

Nick   I love you.

Fran   Is that all you're going to say?

Nick   Yes.

Fran   I hate you. I hate you.

Darling   I won't have this noise. Out. All of you. This is my house. Do what I say.

Exit **Joe** *and* **Martin**.

Frances.

Fran   Go and look at a cow? Am I to go and look at a cow?

Darling   Frances . . .

Fran   That's . . . it's . . . it's . . .

Nick   Fran.

Fran (*shouting*)   No. Don't. Just . . . don't. Fran. Fran. I'm going to bed. I'm going to get into bed.

She waits. Looks at them both. Looks at **Nick**. *Exits.*

Nick   No.

Darling   No?

Nick   Just . . . no.

Darling   I saw you once. I mean, really saw you. And Joe.
It was at the cinema. Such a long time ago. Do you
remember that scene in *Cabaret* when Liza Minnelli and
Michael York stand underneath a railway bridge and she
shouts her head off when a train goes over the bridge and
then she wants him to do it too and he won't but eventually
he does and they do it together? And watching it makes
people laugh because it's so madcap and she's so full of brio
and breathlessness and Michael York is falling in love with
her and her brio despite the stiffness of his breeze and after
all it's happy Berlin just before it's unhappy Berlin. It's a
scene that . . . I looked across at you and Joe and you had
that cinema-is-wonderful look in your eyes . . . all glistening
and light . . . and simultaneously, without looking anywhere
but at the screen, you both popped another Malteser into
your mouths. Anyway, I saw you adoring the grandness of
her gesture . . . what you thought she was doing . . . under
the railway bridge, shouting her head off. I remember how
lonely I felt. Away from you both. She's under a railway
bridge. You can't hear her. No one will hear her. She'll die,
I thought. Shouting won't help. And all you two wanted to
do was shout with her.

Nick   I'm going for a walk.

Darling   All right, Nicholas. Walk. I'll cook. You walk.
Try hard. You know where they all are if you . . . Joe
maybe. Maybe Joe. After all.

Exit **Nick**.

Scene Five

The village cricket pitch.

Joe   Look at it. A place like this. Full of ghosts. Full of silly
mid-offs. Full of . . . old applause. It's better than Upton
Park, isn't it? There are no ghosts at Upton Park. Bobby
Moore is dead and the whole place still smells of *today's*

urine. But here . . . I've been thinking – we should . . . you know how we always talk about it . . . Texas.

Nick   Jesus.

Joe   We should just actually do it. Make a difference. Go to bloody Texas or something.

Nick   Go to bloody Texas.

Joe   A clear and angry mind . . . would be a good thing. It would help, wouldn't it?

Nick   Help? Who? (*Pause.*) Would it?

Joe   Listen. I'm sorry. Do you want to . . .

Nick   No.

Joe   Are you all right?

Nick   No.

Joe   No. What did she mean? Get off the bus?

Nick   God knows.

Joe   Guinness rang. They're beside themselves. We write like angels he says.

Nick   He's right.

Joe   They want more.

Nick   Really?

Joe   Much more. Don't worry – not more of the same. The second half of the book – it's really a whole new book – they want us to stop doing head to heads and switch to subject battles.

Nick   Subject battles.

Joe   That's what he said. So . . . the best song about a given subject.

Nick   Like what? The best *love* song?

Joe   No. They know us now. They've trusted us with the essays. They know what we're capable of . . . the depths we can reach, the connections we can make.

Nick   We're very deep.

Joe   Deep with six 'e's' in the middle.

Nick   A whole line of 'e's' between the 'd' and the 'p'.

Joe   He said . . . actually he laughed and then said . . . no, wait . . . he coughed and laughed and then said: 'Obviously you can't do *love*.' And I think he paused. I think he thought, maybe, I was going to say: 'Oh, yes we can.' He gave me the pause, just in case I was going to say: 'Love? Of course we can do *love*.' Then he laughed again. 'Obviously not,' I said. 'Obviously not,' he said. 'But we could do love in sub-divisions.'

Nick   Brilliant.

Joe   He nearly wet himself.

Nick   Straight into his rock and roll colostomy bag. What sub-divisions were you thinking of? For love.

Joe   Well, there's domestic violence. For example.

Nick   It's a Thin Line between Love and Hate.

Joe   'He Hit Me and It Felt Like a Kiss'.

Nick   'Delilah'.

Joe   'Delilah'?

Nick   Why? Why? Why?

Joe   Delilah.

Nick   She stood there laughing. I felt the knife in my hand and she laughed no more.

Joe   Forgive me Delilah . . .

Nick   I just . . .

Joe   I *just* . . .

Nick   I *just* couldn't take any more. The best domestic violence song?

Joe   Obviously you wouldn't call it that.

Nick   Obviously not. What would you call it?

Joe   Love and Pain or something.

Nick   Or something.

Joe   Martin suggested one.

Nick   Did he?

Joe   A good one.

Nick   A love sub-division?

Joe   No. A whole subject battle. Electric chair songs. The Green Green Grass of Home . . .

Nick   And . . . wait . . . shit . . . wait. Yes. Of course. Terry.

Joe   Goodbye Michelle it's hard to die.

Nick   When all the birds are singing *in* the sky.

Joe   *In* the sky.

Nick   We had joy, we had fun, we had seasons in the sun, but the stars we could reach were just starfish on the beach.

Joe   Look. Up there.

Nick   Twinkle, twinkle.

Joe   Little starfish. Obviously you wouldn't call it Electric Chair songs.

Nick   No. State murder . . . songs.

Joe   Institutionalised killing . . . songs. What are you going to do?

Nick   I don't know.

Joe   No. I can see.

Nick   Can you?
I don't need to go to Texas, Joe. This case . . . heart and
soul . . . you know . . . heart and bloody soul. I mean, the
end of the world and all that . . . but heart and soul. Thank
God. At last.

Joe   Gary Mills got off. In the Mags. Walked out of Bow
Street.

Nick   Really. I'm sorry. Well done.

Joe   Thanks.

Nick   Darling said you. She said I should speak to you . . .
which, given her point of view, what she wants . . . was a
stupid thing to say.

Joe   Completely stupid.

Nick   I mean . . . you, Joe.

Joe   Hopeless. What was she thinking of?

Nick   Old wise tits.

Enter **Martin**.

Martin   Beautiful.

Nick   Jesus. Creeping up like that.

Martin   England. Beautiful. Pure England. Makes you
proud. Don't it?

Joe   Yes. Goodbye.

Martin   I was in the pub . . .

Joe   Are you deaf?

Martin   A chat with the vicar. Like you do.

Joe   Really? Fascinating.

Martin   Mr Page. Would you mind?

Joe   What?

Martin   Go back to the house.

Joe   What?

Martin   Fuck off, sir, can you?

Joe   What?

Martin   Fuck off.

Joe   All right.

Exit **Joe**.

Nick   What is this?

Martin   We belong here, don't we? I mean, you know you're English. Here.

Nick   Get on with it.

Martin   If that's how you want it played.

Nick   Played? Played? Just get on with whatever it is you've got to say.

Martin   Someone was killed.

Nick   What? Who?

Martin   He . . .

Nick   He?

Martin   He. Yeah.

Nick   Where is she?

Martin   She? What she?

Nick   Where is she, Martin?

Martin   Look. The shadows.

Nick   What?

Martin   Ours. All the way across the pitch. Amazing.

Nick You fucking talk to me – now.

Martin Easy. Easy. The vicar was telling me it happened somewhere they call the witches' hole.

Nick Where is she?

Martin Blow to the head. Apparently. Some mad fucking witch probably. Poor fucker. Some stone, some witch . . . I reckon. Turned his lights out. Smacked his head in. No weapon yet. Apparently. And no witch. Stone in pocket, up on the broomstick, off she goes . . . up there somewhere, by now. What do you reckon? What do you reckon, Nick? There she goes. Across the moon. Old skunky cunt.

Nick Shut up. For God's sake, shut up. You're an animal.

Martin No. Well. Yeah. But everyone. Remember. Nicky-boy. Everyone is. Too. Now. It seems to me that Mary might not show up at court tomorrow. What do you think? Maybe a little drugs trial not so upperfuckingmost in her mind any more? And. As well. It seems to me, also, that it would be a bit awkward for you to try and explain to the judge why not. Wouldn't you say? Beats me why she's not here, your honour. I'm as surprised as anyone. Just another client gone walkabout. There we are. There we fucking are, your honour.

Nick I'll be there.

Martin It'll be the last time you work if you are. Get real, Nick. You know the score.

Nick Fuck the score.

Martin No. Not fuck the score. Never fuck the score. Now. Listen.

Nick Martin . . .

Martin (*he punches* **Nick** *twice in the stomach and then holds him*) Fucking shut up. This is it. This is what. Get it in your soft head. Get it hard in your soft head. A bit of this and a bit of that, up there, and then you came home. Right? That is what I believe to have occurred. Am I right. You saw no one. Daddy did not drop into skunky's hole. Did he? (*Shouting.*) Did he?

Nick *is silent.* **Martin** *takes his silence to indicate agreement.*

Martin   Good. I believe you.

He lets go of him.

I believe you. Now all you've got to do is shut up. For always. No more Mary Duggan. End. It finishes here. All right. I love you.

Nick   It finishes here.

Martin   Yeah. Done. Finish.

Nick   I've got my silly head on, Martin. Silly mid-off, fucking stupid mid-on. That's me. Look. Do you see? There I am. That's me. Shouting my head off. For her. Just me. And her. She'll be there. You'll see.

Exit **Nick**.

Martin   Beautiful, though. Beautiful. Fuck it.

He takes out his mobile phone and dials.

Brighton police? Yeah. The Duggan murder. Never mind. Forget the formal crap. Just listen. The daughter. Yeah. Mary Duggan. That's right. Take a look at Mary Duggan . . . and when you do . . . have a look for a stone in a pocket. My name? Verdi. Giuseppe Verdi. V.E.R.D.I. (*Ends call*).

Scene Six

Later that night. **Nick** *alone in the kitchen. Enter* **Darling**.

Nick   Have they charged her?

Darling   I'm doing the first appearance . . . in the morning . . . Lewes Magistrates Court.

Nick   His hand came from out of the blue. And pulled her up. And she had the stone in the palm of her hand and she wanted to . . . Is she all right?

Darling   Where's Fran? You should . . .

Nick   What? I should what?

Darling   Ten years ago someone made me happy, very happy . . . for a year. He took me away from contentment, from a perfectly good, contented life and made me happy. Then he left. It has been very hard getting the contentment back . . . and to be honest I don't think I've done it. I wish I'd never left it. Happiness is much too noisy. I don't miss the happiness. I miss the contentment.

Nick   Don't patronise me.

Darling   I know how fast you think you have been running and how far you've imagined going.

Nick   You look after her. Tomorrow.

Darling   Of course.

Nick   You know what I mean.

Darling   It's my job. It's a case.

Nick   No. It's not a case. It's not a fucking case.

Darling   You're shouting. I'm not going to talk to you if you shout.

Nick   He was a monster – her father. A real monster.

Darling   Maybe he was.

Nick No. Not maybe. He was.

Darling It's a case. It's a first appearance in the Magistrates Court. It's a simple thing. I'll do my job.

Nick You know what tomorrow will mean . . . for Mary. You know very well that it's not a simple thing. And you know what you can do if you want to. They'll bring her out into the light and yours will be the first face . . . you get her up and running. Darling, you make her see what she should see . . . that all this was his fault . . . you get her started on the how and why. He was a monster. A real monster. You do some bloody dancing tomorrow and you get her dancing with you.

Darling Have you talked to Fran?

Nick She's in bed.

Darling Have you talked? No. You're doing this first. What are you doing, Nicholas? Mary Duggan killed her father and now you're even more in love with her. The worse it gets the better it gets. What are you doing? If I were a good Catholic I'd tell you that life is hard and no one said that being married would be easy and in the end if you choose to stay married you'll be a much better man . . . or rather you'll feel yourself to be better because of the hard choice you've made and that's just as good. But in the next hour or so I'm going to slip into bed and wrap my gorgeous legs around another married man and forget . . . forget. So. Don't listen to me. But . . . but, wouldn't it be terrible, darling, if you let Fran go, if you smash it all up and then find you've got it all wrong? It might be a very long wait at the gates of Holloway and it might be for nothing at all.

Nick You don't know.

Darling Of course I know. You're not special, darling. Everyone is doing it. Yours is an ordinary life. Just like mine. You shouldn't . . . you shouldn't give things the words they don't deserve. Mary Duggan is not your tragedy. You love her and it's all blue bloody electric neon, I'm sure, but in five years' time you will have stopped shouting her name from the rooftops and you will have to work out what it all means. Remember ordinary life, whatever you do. Neon looks absolutely hopeless in the morning and morning always comes.

Nick *laughs*.

Nick   She gave her neon speech.

Darling   Her neon-in-the-morning speech.

Nick *begins to cry quietly*.

Darling   I don't trust you when you cry. You should know that, darling.

Nick   She needs looking after. I was doing it. I was looking after her.

Darling   But you weren't listening. You were shouting. And she killed her father. Things get broken . . . when people shout.

Nick   I love her. I love her. That's all. It's simple. What am I supposed to do? It's just called love. What's wrong with that? What the fuck is wrong with that?

Darling   My God, I feel sorry for you.

Nick   I can't walk in a straight line I love her so much. Are you sorry? Yes, I think I can take on the whole of the world. Are you sorry? And I'm fucking mad and I skip and run and dance and splash . . .

Darling (*quietly*)   Listen . . .

Nick   . . . and cry and cry when the ball goes in the wrong end and I cry even more when it goes in the right end . . .

Darling (*a little louder*)   Listen . . .

Nick   . . . and I sing my head off in the bathroom and Luciano Pavarotti breaks my bloody heart and I wish like fuck my father could have sung Verdi on the beach.

Darling (*shouting*)   Listen. (*Quietly.*) You're shouting.

Nick   Yes, I am. At the top of my voice. Are you sorry? Do you feel sorry for me?

Darling (*going to leave*)   But that's not the right question, darling. The right question is what are you going to do? And your answer is that you don't know. Shout that at the top of your voice. (*Leaving.*) Foolish, glamorous noise.

Scene Seven

Enter **Fran***, dressed. She is carrying a carpet bag. She stops. Enter* **Martin** *in T-shirt and boxer shorts.*

Martin   Where's Nick? (*Pause.*) Where are you going?

Fran   In bed.

Martin   Where are you going?

Fran   Asleep.

Martin   It's sorted. I've sorted it.

Fran   You look funny. You look very funny.

She laughs and then cries.

Martin   I'll tell you something . . .

Fran   He knew I was awake. You know, don't you? When someone's awake. He . . . put himself around me and tried to breathe like I was breathing. And now . . . he's asleep.

Martin   It's done with.

Fran   Done with? Is it? 'Stroke my head.' That's what he means. With his getting into bed and his breathing and his going to sleep. Poor Nick. 'Stroke my head.' Night night.

Martin   With Darling . . .

Fran   Darling.

Martin   I've had my face pushed in her places, I mean, right in, as far as it goes, as close as I can be and the smell is thick milk or thick . . . and it's all there is . . . and then, from nowhere, from fucking nowhere . . . the smell of the top of his head. Jake. His head. Whoosh. Blows me away. Kills me. And I hate her. Darling. I love her. But I hate her. And I hate myself. When I smell him.

Fran   Smell him.

Martin   And I don't do it. I don't do anything about it. But . . . and this is it . . . I reckon you might be bigger than what I am. I reckon you might do it, Fran. 'Course he's asleep. Old Nicky. But you knew that. It's no surprise. You've always known. And it won't be a surprise when it's all right either. I've done my sorting. Now it's down to you and whether you're big enough. Be a big girl. Put the bag down.

He comes very close to her. Quietly.

I think you'll be all right. I've got a lot of faith in you, Fran. Put the bag down.

Exit **Martin.**

Very slowly she brings the bag up to her chest and cuddles it. Silent tears.

Scene Eight

Chambers. **Nick** *alone. He puts a tape in the tape-recorder. 'Walk On By'. Enter* **Joe**.

Joe   Lamp-post.

Nick   Lamp-post.

Joe   Lamp-post.

Nick (*quicker now*)   Lamp-post. Lamp-post. lamp-post.

Joe   There goes St Paul's – a mile to the east.

Nick   Swing arms.

Joe   Sing heart.

Nick   The Oxo building.

Joe   Lamp-post.

Nick   The GLC.

Joe   Ken's house.

Nick   Then.

Joe   Now.

Nick   For ever.

Joe   Lamp-post.

Nick   Waterloo Station.

Joe   Lamp-post.

Nick   Waterloo sunset.

Joe   Lamp-post.

Nick   Coin Street.

Joe   Lamp-post.

Nick   The Globe. And there. Charles the Second in a rowing boat.

Joe   Heading for Hampton Court.

Nick   Around dawn.

Joe   Lamp-post.

Nick   Old Vic.

Joe   The Cut.

Nick   Lamp-post. Lamp-post.

Joe   Lambeth Walk.

Nick   St George's Circus.

Joe   Lamp-post. Lamp-post. Lamp-post.

Nick   Sing heart.

Joe   Swing arms.

Nick   Where now?

Joe   Now? Texas.

Nick   Really?

Joe   Really.

Nick   I'll miss you, Joe Page.

Joe   Lamp-post.

Nick   Flying.

Joe   Swing arms.

Nick   Sing heart.

Joe   Where now?

The music stops.

Nick   Elephant and Castle.

Joe   Elephant and Castle. Fuck me.

Nick   Already. I'll miss you, Joe Page.

Joe   Come.

Nick   No.

Joe   Fran? Mary?

Nick   She described things . . . with lots of detail. I
thought it meant she was all right. Time of death. Four a.m.
Checked 3.45 a.m. Asleep. All correct. Fifteen minutes to do
everything and die. I can picture her . . . the way she moved
. . . she must have been cold, getting ready . . . doing
everything. It's slow . . .

Joe   Nick. She was going to plead. She was going to plead
guilty to murder. It's nothing to do with you.

Nick   It's slow because the neck doesn't break . . . under those conditions . . . there isn't far to fall and a sheet won't . . . And she was small . . . so . . . What did her hands do? When she was . . . the time it took . . . what did her lovely hands do? I have dreams . . . . I see her white hands flying about in the darkness in front of my face. Like awful moths. The coroner said three to four minutes. No longer. Three to four minutes. How long is a dream? 'No longer.' About the time it takes to get here.

Joe   Where, Nick?

Nick   Elephant and Castle. At dawn. Swinging. Singing. Where are we? Joe?

Joe   Elephant and Castle. Fuck knows.

Nick *laughs.* **Joe** *laughs. They both laugh.*

Joe   Fuck knows. Nick.

Nick   When you get there . . . Texas. Fucking murder 'em, won't you? I mean . . . really fucking murder 'em.

Joe   Yeah.

Nick   Yeah.

Exit **Joe**. **Nick** *pours a drink and drinks it quickly.*

He puts a tape into the tape-recorder. Joe Cocker – 'With a Little Help from my Friends'. He listens to it. The tape ends.

Fuck knows.

Iona Rain

Iona Rain was first performed at the Warehouse Theatre, Croydon, on 10 May 1996. The cast was as follows:

Bruno Scarrow — Stephen Tindall
Michael Wild — Paul Brightwell
Anne Wild — Fiona Mollison
Mouse — Ian Bailey
George — Robin Hooper

Directed by Jessica Dromgoole
Designed by Anthony Lamble
Lighting by Paul Russell

Act One

Scene One

The main room of a cottage on the island of Iona. The room is simply furnished. An outside door opens straight into the room, another door leads to the rest of the cottage. It is late afternoon. **Bruno** *and* **Michael** *sit in armchairs drinking wine.*

Michael   Maybe he was awake.

Bruno   What?

Michael   Maybe he stayed awake.
Waiting.

Bruno   Waiting. Unbelievable.

Michael (*beat*)   Mouse.

Bruno   The Mouse. (*Beat.*) You said to him once . . .

Michael   Yes.

Bruno   You can have a punch in the face . . .

Michael   God.

Bruno   Instead.

Michael   Instead. God. (*Beat.*) The last time . . .

Bruno   Yes.

Michael   Can you imagine?

Bruno   A mouse never forgets.

Michael   Cheers, Bruno.

Bruno   Cheers, Michael.

They drink.

We bumped into each other in Regent's Park. A chance encounter.

Michael   You sound like . . . is there still all that . . . what do I mean?

Bruno   Yes, Mr Wild, what do you mean?

Michael   Very yellow street lamps and very wet pavements . . .

Bruno   Hugely significant raincoats . . .

Michael   Yes.

Bruno   Collars turned up against the wind and the rain and whatever else might be out there.

Michael   Yes.

Bruno   Yes.

Michael   In the park . . .

Bruno   In the park, in the Rose Garden, he was sniffing an English Holiday.

Michael   Sniffing.

Bruno   For three and a half minutes . . . the same rose.

Michael   What were you doing there, Mr Scarrow?

Bruno   Looking at the very beautiful roses at a very beautiful time of year. As is my wont. Thank you for asking.

Michael   A pleasure. And thank you for being so frank and candid in your reply.

Bruno   A pleasure.

Michael (*beat*)   In the Rose Garden . . .

Bruno   He made a decision. I saw him have the thought. After three and a half minutes he decided to move on to the Sexy Rexys. I was positioned some yards away behind the Audrey Hepburns – I had time to move but I chose not to. I let him see me. Strange thing was . . . no surprise and instant recognition.

Michael   Maybe he'd seen you earlier.
Lurking.

Bruno   No.

Michael   How so sure?

Bruno   I'm an extremely talented lurker and I've
developed a sophisticated sense of the atmospheres people
inhabit.

Michael   And you're a pompous git.

Bruno   And I'm a pompous git.
Naturally, the first thing I looked for was a sense of
grievance.

Michael   Naturally.

Bruno   Naturally.

Michael (*beat*)   And?

Bruno   Unbelievable.

Michael   Unbelievable. Perhaps we didn't . . .

Bruno   What?

Michael   Fuck him up for life.

Bruno   Oh no . . . we fucked him up for life. It's a cross
we have to bear.

Michael   Out of the blue in a rose garden.

Bruno   Twenty years on.

Michael   Having a quiet sniff at the roses.

Bruno   For fuck's sake.

Michael   For three and a half minutes.

Bruno   The same rose.

Michael   For fuck's sake.

Bruno   The human spirit.

They drink.

We went for a cup of tea on Marylebone High Street. He
said: 'Let's go for a cup of tea,' as though he'd been
expecting me all along.
He has a very large handkerchief.
Perfumed. Monogrammed.

Michael   The adult Mouse with a monogrammed
handkerchief.
Imagine.

Bruno   When one zone is snotted over he just moves on to
a whole new zone.

Michael   A clean zone whenever he needs it.

Bruno   Zone after zone.

Michael   It was done with a sense of humour, what we
did to him.

Bruno   It wasn't a dull thing to do.

Michael   We were always laughing.

Bruno   Ironed.

Michael   What?

Bruno   The handkerchief – ironed.

Michael   Wife of Mouse?

Bruno   No wife.

Enter **Anne**. *She is carrying a fish.*

Anne   Big boys' talk?

Michael   Hi, darling.

Bruno   Hi, darling.

Michael   Give us a snog.

Bruno   Give us a snog.

Anne   Can I have a last cigarette first?

She lights a cigarette without putting the fish down.

Michael   Where did you get that very attractive dead fish?

Bruno   It's one hell of a good-looking fish.

Anne   I've been talking to one of the fishermen on the beach.

Michael   Have you?

Bruno   Have you, darling?

Michael   A real one? Did he speak Scottish?

Bruno   Are there barnacles on his bottom?

Anne   I think he rather likes me.

Bruno   What did you talk about?

Anne   Fish . . . mostly.

Beat.

Bruno   You'll be off to cook the supper then?

Anne (*to* **Michael**)   Do you like him?

Michael   Hate the man. Always have.

Anne   Good.

Bruno   But I'm a tragic figure . . . so he puts up with me.

Anne   I'll be in the kitchen if you need me. I'll be wearing a pink apron and a smile.

Michael   What are we having, darling?

Anne   Fish . . . darling.

Exit **Anne**.

Michael   That's her classy broad act.

Bruno   She's good at it. I had thought it would just be you.

Michael   She wanted to come.

Bruno   Of course. She wanted to meet me.

Michael   Still in love with Sandie?

Bruno   Always and for ever. She never left me. Sandie is written across my left ventricle.

Michael   In capital letters.

Bruno   Stapled in gold.

Michael   And the right?

Bruno   Ventricle?

Michael   Yes.

Bruno   Shaw, of course. In bold italics.

Michael   Sandie . . . Shaw. In bold italics.

Bruno   And when my heart beats it's like a steam train of lust. (*The following like the rhythm of a train.*) San . . . die . . . Shaw . . . San . . . die . . . Shaw . . . San . . . die . . . Shaw . . . (*Becoming faster.*) Sandie Shaw. Sandie Shaw. Sandie Shaw. Sandie Shaw. Sandie Shaw. (*Beat.*) And can I say . . .

Michael   Yes.

Bruno   That she's grown more beautiful.

Michael   I think you're right.

Bruno   This is her finest decade.

Michael   By far. And there's so much more to come.

Bruno   Now and for ever.

Michael   Panache.

Bruno   Pure and utter . . .

Michael   Style.

Bruno   The creamy butter . . .

Michael   A vision . . .

Bruno   Of a world without socks.

Michael   You're such a . . .

Bruno   Fan.

Michael   Prat.
You're a lucky man. Having this . . . here.

Bruno   This room – this is where the animals would have been kept at night.

Michael   Shaggy cattle.

Bruno   Yes. Breathing away. Lowing their hearts out.

Michael   And now it's just you – you've evicted the shaggies. An Englishman abroad in the cottage of his dreams . . . breathing away . . . lowing is heart out?

Bruno (*pause*)   Croft.

Michael   Sorry?

Bruno   Croft not cottage.

Michael   Heather not honeysuckle.

Bruno   Exactly.

A silence.

Michael   So . . . three years ago.

Bruno   Easter 1992. Rome. Rome, Italy. Easter.

Michael   So . . .

Bruno   It was vital to Sonia we should go . . . a sort of consecration of my conversion, I suppose. We had to go before . . .

Michael   You can't fly after a while.

Bruno   That's the irony.

Michael   Twenty-eight weeks.

Bruno   Thirty-two. There we were, the two of us, about
to be three, in Pope-town. The convert and the converter.
We spent most of the first day weeping in beautiful
churches. We must have made a strange sight, howling with
happiness in front of stained glass. On the second day she
was in hospital . . . chaos . . . chaos and lights and corridors
and an Egyptian doctor with the smallest hands you've ever
seen. (*Beat.*) Her mother came over. She came from Purley
to Rome and missed her by fifteen minutes.
Missed them.
On the third day I went for a walk, not a walk, a sort of
blunder around. A bright day with big, hard sounds. People
going to work and going to lunch and not knowing . . . with
no idea. I ended up in one of the churches we'd been in on
the first day. And I knew. It was a kind of vision. I stood and
looked at a statue of the Virgin and I knew. No God. (*Beat.*)
My rude awakening I call it.

Michael   Like a morning stiff.

Bruno   What?

Michael   Rude awakening.

Bruno   Jesus.

Michael   Sickening bad taste.

Bruno   Sickening. (*Beat.*) As a matter of fact I did have a
wank – the next morning. I've never been very good at
being alone.

Michael   Jesus.

Bruno   Hated myself, of course.
Capable of anything.

Michael   In the face of such terrible tragedy all he could
do was pull on his penis. Mr Scarrow?

Bruno   Mr Wild?

Michael   What were you doing when Kennedy was shot?

Bruno   When Kennedy was shot I was having a wank.

Michael   At the age of nine he was having a wank. Men pulled over in their cars, women fainted in offices, did masturbators miss a beat? Did they stop altogether? If they stopped, did they resume later?

Bruno   Waiting of course . . .

Michael   For the President to die.

Bruno   As a mark of respect.

Michael   All the young masturbators of '63.

Bruno   God bless them all.

Michael   The long and the short and the tall.

Enter **Anne**. *She is wearing a pink apron and smoking a cigarette.*

Anne   God bless all who?

Bruno   Don't you ever listen before you come into a room?

Anne   Supper will be ready in ten minutes . . . Bruno.

Bruno   Very effective use of the name . . . Bruno. A sour twist at the last, like a sherbet lemon in the mashed potato. But . . . somehow lacking in spontaneity, a whiff of technique about it. Fatal flaw.

Michael   I'll get another bottle.

Exit **Michael**.

A silence.

Bruno   What do you think?

Anne   Of what? (*Beat.*) You won't impress me by being oblique.

Bruno   I'm not being oblique.

Anne   No. You're not.

Bruno   To be fair.

Anne   To be fair. What do I think? At the moment I think you're a complete cunt, but I'm reserving my position.

Bruno   'Eminent' is what they say, isn't it? She's an eminent barrister. The eminent Anne Wild called him a complete cunt. And reserved her position. You look hot and bothered – cooking or temper I ask myself.

Anne   No you don't.

Bruno   No I don't?

Anne   It wasn't . . .

Bruno   . . . something I asked myself at all.

Anne   Quite.

Bruno   For effect only.

Anne   Quite.

Bruno   I'm allowed my moods, a man with my history.

Anne   Yes. Lee-way.

Bruno (*beat*)   Is is a happy marriage?

Anne   It's a marriage.

Bruno   Is it?

Anne   You mean my answer was defensive?

Bruno   Yes.

Anne (*beat*)   Then I forgive you.

Bruno   You forgive me?

Anne   I forgive you your cynicism.

Bruno   She called him a complete cunt but forgave him his cynicism. At the end of the day.

Scene Two

The next morning. **Anne** *and* **Michael** *sit at the table in silence.*
Enter **Bruno**.

Anne   Where's Bruno?

Michael   Out procuring the supper probably.

Anne   Hunter-gathering for his buddy.

Michael   He'll manage to strangle a flatfish or something.
Though I do hear . . . apparently . . . if you flutter your
eyelashes at the fishermen they simply throw fish at you.

Anne   So it's fish again.

Michael   You'll have to do something different with it.

Enter **Bruno**.

Bruno   He's bringing someone.

Michael   What?

Bruno   They got off the boat at Craignure together.
Mouse and a woman.

Anne   Oh, God. A woman. What are we going to do?

Bruno   He was supposed to come alone.

Anne   Well, there we are then, she can help in the kitchen,
whoever she is. How do you know all this?

Bruno   I have friends.

Anne   He has friends.

Bruno   The depths people will go to.

Anne   Depths?

Bruno   I'm going for a walk.

Michael   He said, leaving a thousand questions hanging
in the air.

Anne   They'll be here in an hour.

Bruno   I'll be back in an hour.
The length of the beach – I've timed it – forty minutes out, forty minutes back.

Michael   That's more than an hour.

Bruno   I've deducted ten minutes each way as allowance for the connection between livid thought and livid feet.

Anne *laughs and lights a cigarette.*

Michael   You were in a good mood when you timed it?

Bruno   My mind was ambling and so were my feet.

Michael   He's prone to attacks of ambling, poor man.

Bruno   You'll smell him if he gets here before I get back – money; sanctimony; Philadelphia cheese . . .

Exit **Bruno**.

Anne   I hardly recognise you.

Michael   We have our own way of talking.

Anne   Yes, you do.

Michael   Are you jealous?

Anne   Is that what you want?

Michael   Are you?

Anne   It's just interesting to see you turn into something different. That's all.

Michael   What do you mean?

Anne   Everything goes in his direction – man to man. And I'm left shrieking on the sidelines, or hadn't you noticed? Of course you'd noticed. Michael?

Michael   Sorry.

Anne   I wish you wouldn't do that.

Michael   What?

Anne   Say sorry in the middle of things.
I can't stand it.
And don't go quiet on me. You always make me feel like it's
my fault . . . like I've done something.

Michael   I love you.

Anne   Say something.

Michael   What do you want me to say?

Anne   What you think.

Michael   About what?

Anne   About what I've been saying.

Michael   You're right. I'm sorry. I'll try and . . . I'll try.

Anne   Is he as you thought he'd be?

Michael   It's amazing. All that time and we can just pick
it all up.

Anne   That's good.

Michael   The thing is . . . he's fragile. I know he doesn't
seem . . . he seems . . . hard. But he isn't.
What happened to him . . .

Anne   I don't agree.

Michael   What?

Anne   I don't agree. I think he's . . . not fragile.

Michael   I . . .

Anne (*interrupting*)   You always give people the benefit of
the doubt.

Michael   I can't help that.

Anne   Can't you?

Enter **Bruno***:*

Bruno   I was just outside.

Anne   You didn't go for a walk?

Michael   He stood in the garden and rested his arms on the wall and looked out to sea and every now and again he ran his hands through his hair and sighed into the last of the evening.

Bruno   I was listening at the door as a matter of fact.

Anne   What?

Bruno   I wanted to make sure you were all right.

Michael   Jesus, Bruno.

Anne   Fucking hell. Fucking hell.

Bruno   Are you going to flounce out of the room?

Anne   I don't flounce. As a matter of fact.

Bruno   I'm only concerned for your happiness.

Michael   Listen.

Enter **Mouse** *and* **George** *through the open door.* **Mouse** *is wearing his priest's collar.* **George** *is expensively dressed.*

Mouse. George. Unbelievable.

Bruno   So it's you. The woman is you. Of course.

George   I hope you don't mind.

Bruno   Mind what?

George   I thought since . . . I thought it would be all right to come.

Bruno   Did you?

Mouse   Aren't you going to ask us in?

Bruno   Yes. Come in, Mouse. Come in, George.

A silence.

Michael   Hello, Mouse.

Mouse   Michael.

Michael   Good trip?

Mouse   Yes. Fine.

A silence.

Anne   My name's Anne. I'm married to that one.

Bruno   What were you going to say?

Anne   Sorry?

Bruno   You said I was not fragile? What would you say I was?

Anne   Jesus.

Bruno   So?

Anne   It's very nice to meet you, Mouse, George. I'm going out for a while.

Exit **Anne**.

Bruno   Flounce, flounce.

Michael   She'll be all right.

Bruno   Aren't you going to run after her? Husband.

Michael   She'll be all right.

Bruno   Good.

Scene Three

Bruno *standing by the window. Enter* **Michael**.

Bruno   Is she all right?

Michael   She went for a walk.

Bruno   And she's . . .

Michael   All right. Very touching . . . your concern for our happiness.

Bruno   It's the kind of man I am. How is your happiness?

Michael   All right.

Bruno   That's good.

Enter **Anne**, **George** *and* **Mouse** *together, dressed for dinner.*

Strange miscalculation. Where did you get an idea like that? Any of you. For God's sake. Dressed for dinner.

Michael   For God's sake.

Bruno   And why have you all appeared together . . . coincidence? Or comfort in numbers?

Anne   Should I go first? I'm wearing a little black dress because little black dresses are so . . . classic. I know just what to wear, any time, any place. A little black dress for Iona. Just right. The beach. The sunsets. The sheep. The tiny little black dress. I can't help it. I just get it right.

Bruno   Classy broad.

Anne   And I've worked it out. I think we're here for *Homes and Gardens*. I think we're décor. They're doing a feature. There's a photographer in the rhododendrons.

Bruno   Thank you, classy broad. Mouse?

Mouse   It's what I wear.

Bruno   Yes.

Mouse   The dress options in the church are a bit limiting.

Bruno   Oh no, no, no. Think of the choices. Think of the colours. All that purple. Deep, deep purple. Darkest black with flashing glimpses of white, here at the neck, here at the cuff, like the shifts of a shoal of white-bellied fish in the bottom half of the English Channel. All of that . . . and you have chosen to look like Arthur Askey.

Mouse   Thank you, Bruno.

Bruno   And George? What do we say about George?

Michael   What is there to say?

Bruno   Stunning.

Michael   Fabulous.

Bruno   Enough. No more. That's all that can be said. Adjectives cannot cope.

Anne   Well, that's that then. Can I have I drink?

Bruno   What would you like, wife of my dearest and oldest friend?

Anne   Babycham.

George *laughs a little too abruptly.*

Mouse   Got any beer?

Bruno   In the kitchen. Help yourself.

Mouse *exits and returns with bottle of beer.*

Bruno *opens a bottle of champagne and hands round three tumblers. Only* **Mouse** *is not given one.*

Anne   No Babycham then?

Bruno   Here's to all of you. Welcome to St Columba's Island. May you all leave it infused with its magic. To Iona.

All   To Iona.

Michael   Steve Sweet's English lesson.

George   What?

Michael   I was thinking about it. Reading *King Lear* out loud.

Bruno   The National Anthem.

Michael   You had to do it. Whenever you heard it, wherever you were, whatever you were doing, you had to stand and take your shoes off. Full fucking attention.

Bruno   Bolt upright. Barefooted.

Michael   It came on the radio . . . the workman doing the roof . . . on his radio, in Steve Sweet's English lesson, in the middle of *King Lear*.

Bruno
'I walk along the city streets
You used to walk along with me'

Michael
'And every step I take recalls
How much in love we used to be'

Bruno
'How can I forget you?'

Michael
'When there is always something there to remind me'

Bruno (*joins in on* . . .)
'always something there to remind me'

Michael   You had to do it. You had to. You were Gloucester.

Bruno   And you were a remarkable Fool.

George   I was Cordelia.

Bruno   And Mouse . . .

Mouse   Third servant to the Duke of Cornwall.

Michael   And we stood up . . . the two of us . . . like demented soldiers. And you couldn't deny Sandie . . . even afterwards. If anyone asked you what you were doing . . .

Bruno   What the fuck you were doing . . .

Michael   You had to say. It was the rule. Steve Sweet just looked at us . . . standing there. For a minute and fifty seconds. I think he thought we'd been overcome by it all. It had all got too much.

Bruno   I'd just had my eyes gouged out.

Mouse   'I'll fetch some flax and whites of eggs to apply to his bleeding face. Now heaven help him.'

Michael   Two boys, simultaneously, standing like fuck knows what, in the middle of *King Lear*.

Bruno   His finest moment, he thought. Shakespeare shock. Sick with Shakespeare.

Michael   Why? He said. Twice. Eventually. After a minute and fifty seconds. Why? (*Beat.*) It's Sandie Shaw, sir. It's the National Anthem. The rest of the lesson . . .

George   I remember . . .

Michael   Was turned into a debate about who was the better writer. Shakespeare or Sandie. Deadly serious. Amazing. Did she actually ever write anything?

Mouse   He had a nervous breakdown.

Bruno   Great leather jacket. Famous for his jacket.

Mouse   He's in some sort of a home apparently.

Bruno   Apparently. In a home. With his famous jacket.

George   It's still light.

Mouse   Half past eleven.

Michael   It would change you . . . a thing like that. Darkness and light. The hours. It would change you if you lived here.

Bruno   You should go and look. It's a strange thing. If you look at the horizon just as the light goes . . . the sea and the sky . . . you can't see the join . . . the same colour . . . but the horizon is still there. You don't lose it. You should go and look.

Anne   I'm going.

Michael (*going with her*)   Do you want a coat?

Anne   No. My little black dress is right.

Mouse   I'll come. If you two don't mind.

George *gets up as if to go.*

Bruno   George can keep me company. We've some catching up to do.

Exit **Anne**, **Michael**, **Mouse**.

Still wearing the gloves, I see.

George   Yes. You don't mind me . . . I thought it would be all right to come.

Bruno   The same horrifying disfigurement.

George   They're the same.

Bruno   Old scabby hands.

George   Infantile eczema, Dr Steel said. Twenty-five years ago. (*Beat.*) It's a beautiful place. (*She goes to the window.*) It's sad that the day has to go at all. Look at the sky. It's so big. Mouse says . . .

Bruno   You shouldn't.

George   Shouldn't what?

Bruno   Give him what he wants.

George   I don't understand.

Bruno   He's a bad man. He'll hurt you.

George   I don't believe you.

Bruno   You're not surprised by what I say.

George   Mouse is a good man.

Bruno   He is not a good man. You can trust me.

George   You can't just say those kind of things.

Bruno   I can tell you everything there is to know about the Mouse.

George   I know him.

Bruno   She thought she knew him.
Look at the sky, she said, it's so big.

George   It's not easy for him.

Bruno   And the water is clear and the sand is white.

George   How long have you been here?

Bruno   Sit down. (*She sits.*) October the eighth, 1994. Scott Berg's wedding. You hadn't seen each other since leaving school. *He* recognised *you*. You wore a wide-brimmed hat, red leather gloves to the elbow. You didn't know who he was at first.

George   How do you know this?

Bruno   You talked for hours – the priest and the girl in red.

George   Were you there? I didn't see you.

Bruno   The weekend before he'd been to Milan – a flying visit. He went to see Milan play Juventus at the San Siro.

George   Football.

Bruno   Milan won. Two-nil. The Mouse took a small tape-recorder to the game in his pocket.

George   What tape-recorder? What for?

Bruno   Every Sunday when he's finished popping flesh and blood into mouths he takes off his God-clothes and changes into his number nine shirt. They play the tape – the crowd from the San Siro.
It's a noisy stadium – eighty thousand for a big game.
They like to play the full ninety minutes.
Sometimes it goes to extra-time. More champagne?

George No. They? You said 'they'.

Bruno Yes.

George What? Who are 'they'?

Bruno He asks a member of the choir round. He knows the parents particularly well. As I was saying, he's not a good man.

George I don't know what you are trying to say.

Bruno Don't you? (*Laughs.*)
Do you remember our fifteen minutes of fame?

George Sorry?

Bruno Don't tell me you've forgotten, George. How could you? Summer lawn, long shadows at the end of the day, full bloom of youth.

George I got cramp in my wrist.

Bruno (*laughing*) You should have said.

George You made me keep my gloves on.

Bruno Abysmally insensitive.

George I didn't care.

Bruno Mind you . . . understandable.
Your hands. They were . . .

George Like boiled lobster.

Bruno Is that what we said?

George It's what *you* said.
I'm going to find Mouse and the others. I won't let you do this . . . not now.

Bruno You'll be too late. It's dark. You've missed the moment.

She is leaving.

The number nine shirt. It's much too small for him. He looks very peculiar . . . from a distance.

George   Why are you doing this?

Bruno   The word must be spread. I'm a truth-sayer, George, and the truth must out.

As **George** *is about to leave, the others return.*

George   I was coming to see it.

Mouse   There'll be other nights.

George   Yes.

Mouse   You look a bit pale.

George   The champagne.

Bruno   The champagne? Does champagne make you pale? I'm a bit flushed. Myself.

Anne   We saw it.

Michael   *You* saw it.

Anne   You are right, Bruno. It's there and it's not there.

Michael   It just went dark. That's all.

Anne   I think it's a question of temperament.

Michael   It's either there or it isn't.

Anne   Was there ever any romance in your soul?

Bruno   Once upon a time.

Michael   If you want to see something that isn't there . . .

Mouse   She's right.

Michael   The priest pronounces.

Mouse   It's the wanting to see it. Temperament. Imagination.

Bruno   Are you a good barrister?

Michael   Yes.

Anne   No.

Bruno   Why not?

Anne   You have to sound like them.

Bruno   The things they say . . .

Anne   The things they say. The way they say it. And all that anecdotage.

Bruno   And you can't do that . . .

Michael   It's her crossness that makes her so effective.

Anne   It's not a useful thing . . . being angry. It doesn't help you.

Bruno   Have you always been angry?

Anne   From day one.
I'm more of a cynic now than anything. I was a crusader once. Very fierce. I got off on the wrong footing. My very first Crown Court appearance. I was sitting there and the judge said, 'Is Mr Smith represented?' and I stood up and said 'Yes, your honour.' He completely ignored me and said, 'If he's not represented we'll have to put the case back.' 'But I'm here,' I said. 'I'll stand the case out until after lunch.' And off he went. Eventually the word came back from the court clerk – I was wearing a blue cardigan under my robes and as a consequence I had become invisible to the Learned Judge.

George   I don't understand.

Anne   Nothing but black permitted and strictly no cardigans.

Bruno   I know what you should have done.

Anne   What?

Bruno   You should have called him a complete cunt.

Michael   Women don't use that word.

Beat.

You cried that night.

Anne   Did I? I don't remember.
Frustration I expect.

Michael   In your sleep.

Lights fade slowly to black and come up again slowly.

Mouse   And I didn't die. I knew then that God wanted
me for a purpose.

George   The doctors said it was a remarkable recovery.

Bruno   Something of a miracle by all accounts.

Mouse   It was a word used, loosely of course.

Bruno   Of course. By all rights you should be dead.

Mouse   Yes.

Anne   Well, congratulations.

Bruno   Sonia took me to Lourdes – once upon a time.
There was nothing wrong with either of us, it was a part of
her processing me towards God. Maybe, I don't know, her
superstitious side told her that a precautionary dip would be
a good idea.

Michael   There was a long way to fall, Mr Scarrow.

Bruno   That's the way with happiness, Mr Wild. You
know all about Lourdes, don't you, George?

George   I worked there last summer.

Bruno   A helping hand. A dipper of cripples.

George   Mouse arranged it for me.

Bruno   You didn't go.

Mouse   I have my duties.

Bruno   We had our dip. We laughed about it later.

Michael   More wine, anyone?

Bruno   They tell you to take your clothes off and when you're down to your underpants one of the dippers whips in behind you and wraps a towel around your middle, quick as a flash. Hey, George?

Anne   I think I'm drunk.

Michael   I think you're drunk.

Anne   I thing you're drunk.

Michael   I think I'm drunk.

Bruno   I had my least attractive underpants on. Actually they were my father's. The Colonel's Y-fronts – yellow and billowing with a strip of grey elastic showing at the back.

Anne   Gorgeous.

Bruno   Like wearing a wind sock, Sonia used to say. She was a laugh.
Until she died.
I was embarrassed. I shouldn't have been – the dippers have seen it all, haven't they, George? Underpants from a thousand nations, a million Catholic underpants a year.

Anne   Most of them diseased.

Michael   The underpants.

Anne   No, the Catholics, not the underpants.

Bruno   Can you imagine? Underpant after underpant, fool after fool. (*Shouting.*) Saved! Saved! Bye-bye, tumour! So long, incontinence! Clean! Clean! Ding-dong-ding-dong! I'm clean! I'm clean! Ding-fucking-dong.

Anne   It's all right, Bruno.

Bruno   No. No, it isn't. It's an abomination. It's a terrible lie. (*Whispered.*) For fuck's sake. She was wearing them . . . the day she died . . . she'd forgotten to pack her own . . . She was wearing the Colonel's Y-fronts. We laughed about what a good fit they were – her stomach. She was wearing them.

Michael (*whispered*)   For fuck's sake.

Mouse   You miss her terribly.

Bruno   I don't want to talk about it.

Mouse   You *are* talking about it.

*Mouse leans across the table and touches **Bruno**'s arm.*

Bruno   Don't.

Mouse   You're angry. I understand.

Bruno   What do you understand?

Mouse   Your bitterness, your search for a reason.

Bruno   Leave me alone.

Mouse   I just want to let you know . . .

Bruno   Don't. Don't start with all that quiet voice kind of shit. You of all people.

*Exit **Bruno**.*

Michael   And they all had too much to drink.

Anne   And too much was said.

Mouse (*to **George***)   You look tired.

George   Yes. The air I expect. I think I might . . . good night, everyone.

*Exit **George**.*

Anne   I'm going to bed too. At some stage during the night I think I'll be throwing up. Please don't try and help me, it's all my own fault and I shall bear the consequences bravely and alone.

She tries to stand up and fails.

I've changed my mind. I can't get up . . . your honour.
Forgive me, Father Mouse.
It's so good to have a priest in the house.

A silence.

Mouse (*to* **Michael**)   I hated you. I hated you with all my
heart. My hatred was only outweighed by my self-pity.

Michael   I'm sorry.

Anne   Forgive him, Father Mouse.

Mouse   It could have been stopped. I could have told
someone who would have stopped it, but I didn't. I enjoyed
the attention, I suppose.

Michael   You were a well-known victim.

Mouse   Do you remember . . .

Anne   Do you remember? Do you remember? Hail Mary,
full of Grace.

Mouse   You asked me once – in the library it was – you
said: 'Do you ever wank, Mouse?'
I said I did because I thought it was the best thing to say.

Anne   I'm divorcing you, Michael.
Can you get a divorce on this island or is it too fucking holy?
Sorry, Father. Holy Mary, Mother of God.

Michael   And did you?

Anne   What is wrong with you?

Mouse   I'm ashamed to say that I did.

Anne   Well, I'm glad we've got that cleared up.
Absolutely vital. The priest was a wanker.

Mouse   And you asked me a second question.

Michael   I remember.

Mouse   You said: 'Who do you think about when you do
it?'

Michael   And then I said . . .

Mouse   And then you said: 'Your mother?'

Anne   Very nice. Fucking hell. Hail Mary.

Mouse   And I didn't answer.

Anne   Of course you didn't.

Beat.

And then what happened?

Mouse   He laughed.

Beat.

I did think of someone when I did it.

Anne   What? Did you?

Mouse   It was him. (*Indicates exit.*) I used to think about him.

Anne   You poor bastard. Holy Mary, Mother of God.

Scene Four

The next morning. **Anne** *sits alone at the table. Enter* **George**.

Anne   I haven't been sick yet.

George   Are you going to be?

Anne   It's touch and go.

George   You won't want breakfast then?

Anne   Thank you. No. Is Mouse up?

George   I don't know.

Anne   No.

George   He likes to walk in the mornings.

Anne   I can't remember the last time I had any exercise. I can't remember very much to be honest.
Can't remember . . .

George   Michael was a good runner.

Anne   Was he? Yes. Very sporting, old Michael. Game fellow. (*Beat.*) Were they . . . did they . . .

George   It's a long time ago.

Anne   I apologise on behalf of my husband.

George   He seems like a nice man.

Anne   Is that how he seems?
One forgets to look.

George   He sounds the same.

Anne   There's a word . . . when someone picks up the way someone else talks and adopts it for themselves.

George   I don't know. (*Beat.*) I can't remember what Mouse sounded like.

Anne   You didn't know him then?

George   He was unimportant.

Anne   Not one of the famous ones.

George   No.

Anne   It was better to be famous.

George   It was safer.

Anne   Mouse said something last night about Bruno.

George   What did he say?

Anne   Just how much he thought about him – the victim's love for his enemy, all that . . . the Church was the right place for him.

George   Has Bruno said anything to you about Mouse?

Anne   I think he's got him here to apologise to.

George   Do you think so?

Anne   What exactly did they do to him?

George   You don't know?

Anne   No. Michael hasn't told me.

George   I don't know either.

Anne   Mouse hasn't . . .

George   No. He's a forgiving man, you see. He says it's best I don't know.

Anne   Do you know what I think?
Could you get me a glass of water? (*She does.*)
I wish they were all back there.

George   Even Mouse?

Anne   He's here now, isn't he?
And so are you for that matter.

Beat.

All boys together.

George   And you?

Anne   I'm here because I am the wife of a game fellow who wants to be the same game fellow all over again.

George   You wouldn't be here if you didn't want to be.

Anne   Is that a criticism? Should I not be here?

George   I only meant you seem like someone who makes your own decisions.

Anne   I'm sorry . . . I didn't mean to . . . I am enjoying talking to you. It's a relief.

George   From them?

Anne   Yes. From smartness.

George   I'm used to it.

Anne   But you left all of them . . .

George   And now it's as if I've never been away.

Anne   Did they hurt you?

George   Oh yes.

A long beat.

Anne   And now?

George   You can't just leave that kind of thing alone. The thing is it's not as if they're not paying attention. They spend a huge amount of energy in causing your pain. You do feel that you might be wanted . . . or else . . . why? What would be the point of it all?

Anne   Have you . . . I mean, are you . . .

George   Have I gone all the way? Has a man in a mask with a gleaming knife changed the whole hog? Am I indented?

Anne   You sound like them . . . all of a sudden.

George   There was a night – I was about fourteen – there was some dancing in a dormitory . . . some of them had got hold of something to drink . . . and so they had stopped hating me and they were all looking at me. I was the prettiest, you see. And I felt wonderful. They were dancing around and smashing things on the floor.

Anne   High jinks.

George   Yes. I remember very clearly: Bruno stood in front of me, looking at me in that way of his. I picked up a bucket of water and poured it over him. And everyone stopped what they were doing and looked. (*Beat.*) And he laughed. And I felt wanted. I felt I had got there. And then I was dancing too, flinging myself around, throwing my clothes off, kicking off all my . . . smallness. Michael threw water at me . . . and I felt so grateful. And then I stood on something – it was a broken cup . . . smashed – it went deep into the soft part of my foot. I froze with the pain and just as I froze, Bruno started to pour water from the bucket over my head. He did it slowly . . . it wasn't his fault. He hadn't seen the blood and I didn't cry out. I waited for him to finish. It took an age. And then, when he had finished . . . I screamed. And everything ended and they went back to hating me. I didn't want to scream. I tried hard not to. But I did.

Anne   You haven't, have you? I mean, it's only the clothes.

George   No I haven't. The man in the mask is still behind the screen.

Anne   Not the whole hog.

George   No.

Anne   And will you?

George   I think I'm still screaming. I mean, I don't think it ever stopped. Maybe one day it will all be quiet enough for me to choose . . . once and for all.

Anne   One day. I hope so. Did you go to Lourdes for your hands?

George   I had to keep the gloves on. It wouldn't have been right for people to have seen.

Anne   I'm sorry.

George   Apart from my mother Mouse is the only person I've allowed to put the ointment on for me. I watched his face the first time. He's a good man, Anne.

Anne   I'm sure he is.

Scene Five

Late afternoon. **Bruno** *and* **Michael** *stand on a cliff-top looking out to sea.*

Bruno When I flew back from Rome, without her, with the seat next to me empty – paid for and empty . . . it was a good flight. I mean the actual flight. You know how I hate flying. It was a very smooth flight. Very. Just for a moment I thought . . . someone was making it easier for me. Pathetic. A pathetic thought.

Michael He creeps back in? From time to time.

Bruno We flew from Luton . . . to Rome. I took the train into Luton from the airport when I got back. I wanted to be somewhere . . . the opposite of Rome. Luton is . . . have you been there? Completely . . . there is no God in Luton. Luton was what I wanted. There's a Tourist Information Office near the station. There was a poster in the window: 'The Changing Face of Luton', it said. I stood and looked at it and I sort of crumpled. I think I curled up on the pavement. I wasn't laughing and I wasn't crying. It was both at once. A police officer with a beard came and picked me up. 'Where are you going?' he said. Where am I going? What kind of question was that from a police officer with a beard, with a helmet on, in Luton.

A silence.

The Vikings were here. A thousand years ago. Picture the horror. Square sails appearing. A glint of metal in the sunlight. Horn-heads. And what is there? Three square miles of island and no trees.

Michael What's a man to do?

Bruno Hot foot it into the monastery and hope like hell Eric got out of bed on the right side. Sixty-eight monks murdered – down there – one morning in AD 803.

Michael Do you suppose they put up a fight?

Bruno   They didn't. Extraordinary courage – just to die. To stand on a beach and wait to die.

Michael   Do you remember the bleedings?

Bruno   God. Yes. The bleedings.

Michael   Penknives across thumbs.

Bruno   Clean cuts. Bright blood.

Michael   Skin flaps.

Bruno   Yes. Monstrous, really.

Michael   Really.

Bruno   Half the school had their thumbs slit open.

Michael   By us.

Bruno   By you.

Michael   What?

Bruno   You did the cutting.

Michael   Did I?

Bruno   Yes. You did. Bastard.

Michael   And you . . .

Bruno   I stood and watched . . . with horror . . . your deadpan violence. Scarred for life.

Michael   I suppose so.

Bruno   No. *Me*. Scarred for life. Bastard.

Michael   Sorry.

Bruno   Bastard. What does Anne make of me?

Michael   Is it important?

Bruno   She's your wife. What does she say?

Michael   Not much.

Bruno   Eloquent silence.

Michael   Or something.

Bruno   The weather is lovely.

Michael   Sorry. She's a bit thrown, I think.

Bruno   I said the weather is lovely.

Michael   She's scared of you.

Bruno   She doesn't seem scared.

Michael   Lost soul, Bruno. Fucked up and adrift. Anne has a preference for certainties. Firm ground.

Bruno   The convent girl with leftover business.

Michael   Something like that. She can't pin you down.

Bruno   I'm a problem.

Michael   Are you?

Bruno   You know I am. So are you, Michael. I can't understand why she married you.

Michael   That boat . . .

Bruno   Wallace. He has a lot of sheep on the island. People laugh at him because he spends most of his time on his boat. I know why he's out there. His boy fishes from the rocks at the end of the beach. He's keeping an eye.

Michael   Anne says we're trying to reclaim a time when we were all in the thick of things.

Bruno   Does she? Do you think it can be done? A thing like that?

Michael   You have your anger.

Bruno   And what shall I do with it? Answer me that. There's a hole in my bucket, dear Michael.

Long beat.

Somewhere down there in the sand is thousand-year-old blood. Imagine.

Michael   Have you ever . . .

Bruno   . . . killed anyone? I've had it done. There can come a time when it's down to percentages.

Michael   The weather, as you were saying, is lovely.

Bruno   If killing a man means others are kept from harm then it should be done. It must be done.

Michael   Irrespective of the quality of the men. When you were . . .

Bruno   Yes?

Michael   Before Sonia died . . .

Bruno   When I was?

Michael   Talking to God.

Bruno   We hadn't started that particular discussion.

Michael   Were you going to?

Bruno   I was happy.

Michael   You didn't stop to think?

Bruno
  Away in a manger
  No crib for his bed
  The little Lord Jesus
  Laid down his sweet head.
Simple and sweet, Michael.

Michael   And now?

Bruno   And now . . .

A silence.

On the beach.

Michael   They could be lovers out for a stroll.

Bruno   He moves very easily for such a large man. No apology for his size.

Michael   It's cold.

Bruno   The wind.

Michael   Does the beach have a name?

Bruno   Martyr's Bay.

Lights fade down and come up again on **Mouse** *and* **George** *on the beach.*

Mouse   They died simply, at prayer.

George   Was it here? Were they killed here?

Mouse   Hereabouts.

George   When I was eight years old my father took me to the battlefield at Culloden, only he didn't tell me where we were going beforehand. It was February, I remember. My ears hurt and my feet hurt. We stood in the middle of a field and I looked down at a puddle and he said: 'What do you feel?' I started crying. I didn't know why. I didn't know where I was. There are places . . . he gave me his handkerchief. There are places . . .

Mouse   If we have time I'll take you to Eileach an Naoimh.

George   What is it?

Mouse   It's an island in the Garvellochs, off Islay. There was a monastery there too. All that's left are the tiny drystone monks' cells.

George   You've been there?

Mouse   I've wanted to for a long time.

George (*beat*)   Think of it . . . hundreds of miles in their boats to kill good men in cold blood.

Mouse   What does that tell you about the power of the victims?

George   The murderers were scared.

Mouse   They were terrified. They didn't understand and so they tried to kill what they didn't understand.

George   Sometimes, when I need to, I think about the time it's all taken, the weight of history, and how small I am . . . and it reassures me.

Mouse   We all have doubts.

George   I didn't mean . . . Do you?

Mouse   After Mass I make a point of spending time alone. It's important to administer to yourself when you've finished administering to others.

A silence.

Mouse   You know, you should stop wearing those gloves.

George   It's not easy.

Mouse   I know. But you should stop wearing them. Let me. (*He takes her gloves off and holds her hands in his.*) They're beautiful hands.

George   Look. Bruno and Michael. On the cliff.

She waves briefly and then puts her hands behind her back.

We should have . . . at school, I mean . . . we could have helped each other.

Mouse   We were much too busy aspiring to be like them. Rubbing shoulders with other weaklings wouldn't have helped.

George   What they did . . .

Mouse   I've told you . . . it's unfair to label them. I won't do it.

George   I'm sorry. I didn't mean to make you angry. He hasn't changed – Bruno.

Mouse   He's capable of changing, as we all are.

George   I think he's finished.

Mouse   Finished? What on earth do you mean?

George   I thinks he's dangerous.

Mouse   He's bitter and he's angry and he needs help, which is why I'm here.

George   To help him?

Mouse   He lost his faith and he wants it back.

George   Be careful.

Mouse   It's my job.

George   It's funny when you call it a job.

Mouse   George. You shouldn't have too much respect for me. I'm not someone to follow.

George   Is that what you think I want?

Mouse   It's not easy.

George   To love me?

Beat.

Mouse   It's getting cold.

George   I hadn't noticed.

Mouse   We should say a prayer. For the men who lost their lives here – on this spot – and for the men who took them.

They kneel. Lights fade down on **George** *and* **Mouse** *and come up on* **Bruno** *and* **Michael** *on the cliff-top.*

Michael   Look now.

Bruno   They're praying.

Michael   What do you think they're praying for?

Bruno   The soul of Bruno Scarrow, among other things.
Hello, Lord, how the hell are you? I'm fine. This is George,
he's a good-looking girl, wouldn't you say? A friend of mine,
a child of the Church. About last Sunday. Sorry. I was
tempted and you know how it can get . . .

Michael   What did you do last Sunday, my son?

Bruno   Oh . . . the usual Sunday thing.

Michael   And remind me what that is, my son.

Bruno   Ask Bruno Scarrow, he'll let you know. He knows
all about it.

Michael   Bruno?

Bruno   You'd make an excellent God, Michael. Easy to
talk to.

Michael   Then talk to me.

Bruno   There's nothing to say.

Scene Six

The cottage. **Anne** *sits at the table examining three separate packets of*
condoms. Enter **George**.

George   Hello. Mouse is still on the beach. I'm not
disturbing you?

Anne   I have a decision to make.

George   What are you doing?

Anne   Banana flavour, rib-ticklers or Glo-in-the-dark?
What do you think? I couldn't make up my mind so I
bought them all.

George   Where did you get them?

Anne   The Gents lavvy in the bar at the St Columba
Hotel. The last unholy place before America.

George   You went into the men's toilets?

Anne   Sometimes a girl doesn't have a choice. There was
someone in there actually. A man in a kilt at the urinal.
Gordon.

George   Gordon?

Anne   The tartan.

George   Oh yes. What did he say?

Anne   He was mid-flow.

George   How do they manage?

Anne   With the kilt? Hoick it up with the left hand leaving
the right hand free . . . to . . . shake, rattle and roll. And
sometimes, apparently, they can even talk at the same time
. . . so I'm told.

George   Of course, they could just . . . sit down to do it.

Anne   Men.

George   Men.

Anne   Hopeless.

George   Bless them.
I had a kilt.

Anne   Did you?

George   My first time out of trousers. I always sat down.

Anne (*beat*)   Do you dream about the past?
I only dream about the past. I have a recurring dream – it
comes whenever I sleep in a new place. There I am, aged
fourteen, flat out and face down, stark-naked on the floor of
the dormitory paying for my sins. Around dawn I fall asleep
and one of the other girls puts a blanket over me. I can see
her doing it and I want to tell her to stop but I can't speak

and she puts the blanket around me and her kindness
destroys my pain.

George   At fourteen . . . what were the sins?

Anne   Nothing out of the ordinary.

George   Your honour.

Anne   Your honour. (*Beat.*) But you paid for them,
whatever they were. If you wet the bed as I did, as so many
did, you had to carry the soiled sheets around with you the
following day. Rows and rows of girls clutching pissed-on
sheets to their little flat chests. Breathing in urine. Soaking
up Trollope. Those were my English lessons. Imagine. As
Bruno might say.

George   Unbelievable as Michael might say.

Anne   For fuck's sake.

George   For fuck's sake.

Anne   Trollope.

George   For God's sake.

Anne   And urine.

George   Trollope and urine. Imagine.

Anne   What are you hoping for, George?

George   What do you mean?

Anne   With Mouse?

George   He's kind to me.

Anne   Is that all? Is that all you need?

George   I don't know.

Anne   Is he all right?

George   He doesn't say.

Anne   Don't you have your own idea?

You shouldn't sacrifice yourself, George.

George   Don't be angry with me.

Anne   I'm sorry. You've had a lot of that.

George   I can't pray any more. I go through the motions but it's not praying.

Anne   Have you talked to Mouse about it?

George   I can't.

Anne   Do you think he knows anyway?

George   He trusts me. He takes me at face value.

Anne   I never told anyone. My lapsing took years and I did it all by myself. A slow thaw.

George   And are you . . . ?

Anne   Yes. Lapsed not lapsing.

George   When did it start?

Anne   I was one hell of a good Catholic. The whole thing . . . straight through puberty without even a sideways look at a gymkhana or anything more. Intacta in all respects. I can see it now. I can feel it now. Thin and fierce and shot through with God. Barefooted Annie would have give anything to cut open her foot like you did. Scream? I wouldn't have said a thing.

George   And . . .

Anne   Things change.

George   Tell me how long it has taken.

Anne   I think I'll take a chance with the Rib-ticklers. What do you think?

George   Why don't you ask Michael?

Anne   Why?

George   Well . . .

Anne   Nothing to do with him. He's been out of commission for years. Limp tackle. I'm going to ask my fisherman friend to tickle my ribs.

George   I'm sorry.

Anne   What for? (*Beat.*) Don't be sorry, there's no need.

George   I just meant . . . be careful.

Anne   That's what these are for.

She puts condoms in her pocket.

Enter **Bruno** *and* **Michael**.

Bruno   We decided against it.

George   We saw you from the beach.

Bruno   For a moment . . . at the edge . . .

George   Mouse said you looked like a pair of lemmings.

Bruno   Just for a moment . . . but then you waved . . . it wouldn't have been fair to disturb your little prayer.

George (*laughing suddenly*)   You did look a bit like lemmings.

Bruno   Lemmings jump in order to get to the other side.

Michael   Very profound, Mr Scarrow.

Anne   Riddle-shit.

Michael   What?

Anne   Men and riddles.

Michael   What?

Anne   Playing in the dark. Do you think it's clever?

Michael   What are you talking about? Riddles?

Anne   Ask Bruno.

Bruno   She thinks people should talk to each other. She thinks people should say what they mean.

Anne   I think wit is an overrated virtue and I think men use it to control conversation. Riddle-shit. Wit-crap.

Michael   What brought this on?

Anne   'What brought this on?'
'What brought this on?'
How far away you seem sometimes.
What does it matter? Think what it's like in the darkness –
for the others.

Bruno   And what is it like?

Anne   Blackness and then sudden violent light and then blackness again. Snap. Black. Snap. Black. Snap.

Michael   Anne?

Anne *lights a cigarette.*

George   Mouse isn't like that.

Anne   No, he isn't.

Bruno   Do you mean that, George?

George   Yes.

Bruno   Think carefully.

George   Yes.

Enter **Mouse**.

George   You're wet.

Bruno   We were just talking about you.

Mouse   The spray. I went all the way to the end of the beach . . . there are some rocks . . .

Bruno   George was saying you always say what you mean.

George   Go upstairs and change. I'll bring you a hot drink.

Exit **Mouse**, *followed by* **George**.

Bruno   You don't mean it, do you, George?

Anne   Leave her.

Bruno   You don't know . . .

Anne   I know cruelty when I hear it.

Exit **Anne**.

Beat.

Michael   Drink, anyone?

Bruno *nods*.

Michael   Do you want to tell me?

Bruno   What?

Michael   The story.

Bruno   What story?

Michael   Or the plan maybe.

Bruno   You'll have to be a little clearer, Michael.

Michael   It's very nice of you to ask us here. Very nice.
But it's one hell of a weird summer holiday. I mean . . . you
know . . . where's the Ambre Solaire? For instance. I don't
know, Bruno, we've been here . . . not long . . . and one
thing is clear: you'd have to be born here to want to live
here. Or . . .

Bruno   Or?

Michael   Mouse. George. Not necessarily the ones you'd
choose.

Bruno   No.

Michael   To reunite with.

Bruno   Not necessarily.

Michael   Not really bosoms.

Bruno   No.

Michael   So what's the purpose? Behind this completely crap summer holiday?

Bruno   Mouse's big friend. Do you remember?

Michael   Haig.

Bruno   Letter-writing. He always wrote the same thing: Dear Mum, How are you? I'm fine. Love, Haig. He thought he was supposed to use his surname for fuck's sake, to his mum. Can you imagine what she thought?

Michael   Broke her heart probably.

Bruno   Probably.

Michael   He had a dad.

Bruno   Dear Mum though. Love Haig. I asked him why he didn't use his first name. He looked at me with a sort of terror. Eight years old.

Michael   Maybe he didn't hear you.

Bruno   Plugs Haig.

Michael   Big plugs. I mean, the whole ear was a plug. Pure plugs. Profoundly deaf. His dad wrote to him. In the guise of the family dog.

Bruno   Yes.

Michael   They took me for a long walk today. I found an old bone and lay down with it in a big, muddy puddle. Lots of love, lick lick, woof woof. Bonnie.

Bruno   Jesus, Bonnie.

Michael   Poor old Haig. Breaks your heart.

Bruno   What do you think he's doing now?

Michael   Don't know.

Bruno   Probably a fuck sight more than you.

Michael   What?

Bruno   What?

Michael   What do you mean?

Bruno   What have you actually done?

Michael (*beat*)   Nothing. in reality.

Bruno   In reality.

Michael   On balance.

Bruno   In reality, on balance . . . nothing.

Michael   Not . . . anything real. Since then.

Bruno   Sad old bastard.

Michael   So brutal.

Bruno   Brutal but true.

Michael   It all went quiet.

Bruno   Totally silent.

Michael   Yes. Deaf-land.

Bruno   And dumb.

Michael   Deaf and dumb. Just a faint humming.

Bruno   Easy listening.

Michael   Yes.

Bruno   James Last. Engelbert.

Michael   Like a sad old Labrador.

Bruno   Like a sad, old, deaf Labrador.

Michael   Called Engelbert.

Bruno   With slippers on. Lick lick.

Michael   Woof woof.

Bruno   Bonnie.

Michael   Jesus.

Bruno   How are you . . . otherwise?

Michael   You're a clever bastard, Bruno Scarrow.

Bruno   Why do you say that, Mr Humperdinck?

Michael   You end up asking the questions.

Bruno   Do I?

Michael   And not answering mine.

Bruno   You're right.

Michael   And?

Bruno   I've still got it.

Michael   What?

Bruno   Wait there. Don't move.

Bruno *goes to the record-player. 'Always Something There to Remind Me' plays.* **Michael** *smiles, takes his shoes off and stands to attention.* **Bruno** *– upstage – does the same. During the course of the song* **Michael** *stays rigidly standing to attention. Very slowly* **Bruno** *softens his stance until eventually he stands easy. Just before the end of the song his picks up his shoes and exits.* **Michael** *does not see him go.*

Michael (*as song ends*)   Excellent. So fucking excellent.

Scene Seven

Night. **Anne** *stands alone at the window. She is wearing a coat. Enter* **Bruno** *(from outside). He doesn't see her until she speaks.*

Anne   Hello.

Bruno   Hello. Where are you going?

Anne   Been. (*Beat.*) You?

Bruno   There's a place I go.

Anne   Are you going to tell Auntie Annie?

Bruno   Across the rocks at the far end of the beach there's a cove and at the base of the cliff there's a cave – more a hole, really. When the tide's out . . .

Anne   And that's where you go? At night?

Bruno   What about you?

Anne   I've been humiliating myself.

Bruno   Are you going to tell Uncle Bruno?

Anne   I don't know his name. He won't tell me. The fisherman – I asked him to tickle my ribs.

Bruno   Jock. His name is Jock Wallace. He's not a fisherman. His boy fishes; it was a fish his boy caught that he gave you.

Anne   My God, I've had my tits squeezed by a man called Jock.

Bruno   Somebody's got to do it.

Anne   Michael's been talking to you.

Bruno   Boys' talk.

Anne   He hasn't got any other friends. He's glad to have you again.

She looks down at her body.

Jock of Iona was here.

Bruno   How are your ribs?

Anne   Untickled. He . . . he started crying, actually. He put his hands here (*She cups her breasts.*) and then cried like a baby for a long time. I have no idea why.

Bruno   Are you all right?

Anne   That's a friendly thing to say.

Bruno   We have things in common, you and I.

Anne   Michael.

Bruno   Michael. He's lost some of his spirit, or spunk as my mother would say.

Anne   That's probably my fault. I think I've sort of eaten him up. Do you talk to him about me?

Bruno   Yes.

Anne   What does he say?

Bruno   Do you want to know?

Anne   No. You're right. I don't want to know. (*Turning to the window.*) The northern sky . . . I've been forgetting to look at it.

Bruno
   Seachd bliadnha roimh 'n bhrath
   Thig muir thar eirinn ri aon trath
   's that Ile ghuirm, ghlais
   Ach snambaidh I chalium chleirich

Anne   Are you being nice to me?

Bruno   An island formed in the morning of the world and destined to be the last place at the world's end.

Anne   There were sheep on the beach today. Lots of sheep on the beach. Funny.
You want me to say that I'm down there with you, don't you? I've stopped feeling sorry for myself.

Bruno   And I haven't?

Anne   What's in it for me, talking to you?

Bruno   You've been out having your tits squeezed by a man called Jock.

Anne   And you've been sitting in a hole at the bottom of a cliff in the middle of the night.

Bruno   As I said – we have things in common.

Anne   He couldn't talk. He was just sobbing and clutching on to me. Poor man.

Bruno   We had a name for the baby – Kevin. There's Kevin kicking we'd say. Goofing around in mummy's tummy – our Kev. They put Kevin in the hospital incinerator. He was a boy. I made them tell me. Ripped out of her and thrown in the fire. What happens? What happens to baby souls who go straight in the fire? What did they tell you at the convent, Anne? What did the sisters say about that?

Anne   Don't shout at me.
Could you get me a drink please.

Bruno   Whisky?

Anne   Fine.

Bruno *gets two drinks.*

Anne   I'm something of a cliché.

Bruno   Most of us are.

Anne   Don't be clever with me. I'm so tired of cleverness. Just let me tell it and don't say anything.

She lights a cigarette.

Twenty-five years ago. They came for me very early. It was still dark. 'Put your dressing-gown on,' they said. And we walked in silence down all those corridors to the Mother's office. Only the sound of soft shoes on stone . . . no one said a word. I was hoping the other girls had woken and seen me summoned . . . and I was hoping it would be something awful. And it was. 'Sit down,' she said. She'd taken her glasses off. I'd never seen her without her glasses. Perhaps she thought it would bring her closer to me. It was as though I was seeing her for the first time. She looked at me for a long time before saying anything and in that time I thought: I hope it's my parents, I hope I'm alone now, I hope it's that awful.

'It's your parents,' she said. And then she put her glasses back on and her face blurred again . . . and I didn't hear much of the rest. (*Beat.*) My mother had given me a pumice stone at the end of the last holiday . . . it was my only real possession . . . there, at the convent.

I had a bath that night . . . dispensation. And I had my pumice stone . . . and I started on myself . . . and I rubbed and rubbed with my eyes closed tight and the water turned . . . a very beautiful colour. I was so thin, it was easy to get through to . . . the blood came easily.

I spent a week in hospital. I think they sedated me . . . I don't remember much. And when I came round I came round with no God. Or at least the idea of no God. The thing was . . . the thing is . . . I think about how they saw me – my mother and father . . . what I was to them. What was I? White-boned, fish-eyed, oh so fascinated with myself and such a long, long way away from them. And then they died. And I'm stuck with that. There's no room for improvement. I can't get them to see me in any other way. She gave me a pumice stone . . . it was all I would take from her. But I'm all right. I'm not down there now. I'm better and better . . .

Bruno   Are you?

Anne   Better and better.

Bruno   Really?

He takes hold of her hands and then moves his hands to her upper arms. Then he kisses her. The kiss is long and fierce and desperate.

Act Two

Scene One

Morning. The cottage.

Mouse   Tonight's the night.

Michael   Josephine. What night?

Mouse   The feast of St Columba.

Anne   Is there such a thing?

George   Sort of. Mouse has decided there is. He thinks the ninth of June was the date he landed.

Mouse   It was the date he landed. I've worked it out very carefully.

George   So, we've decided to make a feast of it tonight.

Mouse   Sixth-century fare – fish, bread, meat, wine – all the basics and lots of them.

Anne   Sounds wonderful, Mouse.

Mouse   Mr Wallace is donating the meat – fresh lamb.

Anne   Is he?

Bruno   Is Wallace coming?

Mouse   I didn't ask. I suppose I should have done.

Bruno   You're paying him for the meat, I hope?

Mouse   I hadn't thought.

Bruno   The world isn't like that.

Michael   The gates of heaven.

Bruno   What?

Michael   Wallace. He can see that Mouse is a priest –
perhaps he needs someone to put in a good word for him.

Anne   For God's sake. Why is everyone calling him
Wallace, like he's someone's butler or something.

Michael   What is his name?

Anne   Jock. His name is Jock.

Beat.

Bruno   I'm going over to St Odhran's.

Anne   The graveyard?

Mouse   Where ancient kings are supposed to lie.

Bruno   Where they *do* lie.

Mouse   I think that's very doubtful.

Bruno   It's not doubtful.

Mouse   Well . . .

Bruno   It is not doubtful.

George (*to* **Mouse**)   We have a lot to do.

Mouse   No time for idle chit-chat.

Anne (*to* **Bruno**)   I'll come.

Bruno   Michael?

Michael   You two go. I'm going to sit here and try and
remember what Camden High Street looks like. Where the
ancient drunks lie. Don't you miss proper life, Bruno? Dog
turds – God, I miss dog turds. Pigeons and vomit on
pavements, pavements, pigeons eating vomit on pavements.
I can almost smell it. If I close my eyes and inhale deeply
I'm back there in the world of stink and noise.

Anne   Where you belong, darling.

Michael   Absolutely where I belong. Where we all
belong. Where there's a George on every street corner and

nobody bats an eye. Don't you just long to brush up against a perfect stranger and come away with your pockets empty? Bump and bang and slap and crap instead of all this peace and quiet and hum and ha. And the bloody wind in your head on this island. My God, I miss the green sky. How long are you holed up for, Bruno? Are you holed up? What *are* you doing here in never never land? Exactly. And who are you? Actually.

Bruno   It depends.

Michael   It depends. My God, he's a worry. This man needs help, Father Mouse. Are you in hiding? Are there people who will stop at nothing to get at you?

Bruno   I don't suppose you'd consider shutting the fuck up?

Michael   I think we have a right to know. If he is in hiding from a serious and evil terrorist threat I want to know. Who is after your blood, Bruno Scarrow? Give us a clue. Who should we be on the lookout for? Pencil-thin Arabs? Desperate women from Stuttgart? Young Americans with blue blue eyes and red red necks? Friends of Frank Sinatra?

Bruno   Shut the fuck up.

Michael   Shut the fuck up again? Very touchy, Mr S.

Anne   Let's go.

Anne *and* **Bruno** *start to leave.*

Michael   I'll stand in the corner for the rest of the lesson, hands on head, blinking back the tears.

Bruno   Good idea, Michael.

Michael   Oh . . . and Bruno? The weather is lovely.

Bruno   Yeah. Isn't it just.

Scene Two

St Odham's graveyard. **Bruno** *and* **Anne** *stand looking at the ground.*

Bruno   It's here. The first burials were there – we know that – and the last, over there. So they're here – under our feet.

Anne   Side by side.

Bruno   One followed the other with no one in between. It makes sense that they'd be next to each other. I wanted to show you. Interesting, don't you think?

Anne   Interesting? Duncan and Macbeth under our feet. Interesting?

Bruno   And so we stand on ancient ground resonant with the bickering of warrior bones. The broken man and the broken woman all aquiver with who knows what. Ankles snap. Knees slip. All is out of joint.

Anne   Better. Kiss me.

Bruno   It doesn't mean anything.

Anne   Yes it does.

Bruno
    The sun shone
    As it had to on the
    White legs disappearing into the
    Green water.

Anne   You have to go on.

Bruno
    The dogs go on with their
    Doggy life.

Anne   Kiss me.

Bruno   And the torturer's horse scratches its innocent behind on a tree.

Anne   Kiss me. Come here.

Beat.

Look at me.

Bruno (*not looking at her.*)   It's a disappointing reality.
Duncan at the head of one army, Macbeth at the head of
the other. The battle of Bothngouane. Duncan was killed –
not by Macbeth, by someone else. He was about twenty-five
years old. That's it. (*Beat.*) I'm sorry.

Anne   Are you *not* kissing me?
Can't we see if our hearts will heave?

Bruno   I'm not worth it.

Anne   Isn't that for me to say?

Bruno   No. It's for me to say. I have to be honest with
myself.

Anne (*laughing suddenly*)   You're so pompous sometimes.

Bruno   There. I heard it.

Anne What?

Bruno   You said you loved me. I heard it. Look.

Anne   Vikings.

Bruno   On a Caledonian Macbrayne ferry.

Anne   Shall we hide?

Bruno   There's nowhere to go. Three square miles of
island and no trees.

Anne
    And the expensive delicate
    ship that must have
    seen something amazing,
    a boy falling out of the sky,
    Had somewhere to get to
    and sailed calmly on.

Kiss me.

Bruno   What about the Vikings?

Anne   Bugger the Vikings.

Anne *kisses* **Bruno**.

Scene Three

The cottage. Early evening. **George** *is finishing setting the table.*

George   Boy. Girl. Boy. Girl.

She sits down at the head of the table and takes her gloves off slowly and deliberately.

Enter **Mouse**.

Mouse   It looks wonderful. You've done a grand job. A toast – before the others get here. To St Columba and the start of it all.

They raise their glasses.

You've . . .

George   Yes.

Mouse   I'm very proud of you.

George   Don't make a fuss, will you?

Mouse   No, of course not.

George (*beat*)   Thank you.

Mouse   What for?

George   Just thank you.

Enter **Bruno** *and* **Anne**.

Anne   Look at this.

Mouse   We had begun to think we were going to have to eat it all ourselves.

Bruno   We've been treading on people's graves.

Anne *laughs*.

Anne   He's so ridiculous.

Enter **Michael**.

Michael   You've taken your gloves off.

George *puts her hands under the table then takes them out again.*

Bruno   We saw Wallace.

Mouse   Good.

Bruno   He said you'd been speaking to his boy?

George   Have you?

Mouse   Yes.

George   What about?

Bruno   Wee laddie Wallace is a bit of a problem. He's fourteen and all he can do is fish. He won't speak to anyone, he wears the same clothes all the time and he just wants to be fishing. I understand you've promised to see what you can do.

Mouse   That's right. I'm . . .

Bruno   In exchange for one of Wallace's lambs. A lamb for a lamb. Very good of you, Mouse, you being off-duty and all that.

Mouse   I'm never off-duty.

Bruno   Oh yes, you have a responsibility to all of the world all of the time wherever you are.

Mouse   Something like that.

Bruno   Exactly like that.

George   Do you remember Bass Roberts and the duck.

Bruno   Yes, George.

Beat.

Anne   What happened?

Michael   In the middle of the night, all by himself, Bass Roberts went to the local park, scaled a wall or two, waded into the middle of a pond, caught a duck and wrung its neck with his bare hands. He brought it back in his wash-bag. He was discovered the next night down by the stream . . .

Bruno   Not far from Victoria Falls . . .

Michael   . . . just down from Lake Superior, lighting a fire to cook the duck in. He'd plucked it on his lap under the desk in double chemistry. He would have been expelled but he was diagnosed diabetic two days later and that saved him. They said he must have had a craving.

Bruno   Why do you mention Bass Roberts and the duck, George?

George   I don't know. Silly. It came into my mind.

A silence.

Mouse   A toast. To the island of Iona.
Thank you for asking us, Bruno.

All raise their glasses apart from **Bruno**.

Anne   Thank you for asking us, Bruno.

Bruno *raises his glass.*

Anne   I've seen him on the rocks at the end of the beach. He's small for fourteen.

Bruno   He puts all the fish he catches back – apart from one each day. He gives one fish a day to his dad.

Anne   Poor soul.

Michael   He just likes fishing. I can think of worse things to do with your adolescence.

Bruno   He's closed down. Silent of voice and silent of everything else.

George   Mouse will talk to him.

Mouse   I'm trying.

Bruno   Tell him you're an angel from Gloucestershire, that'll impress him.

Lights fade down and back up again.

Michael   Mr Scarrow – an explanation.

Bruno   What?

Michael   You'd have us all believe you're having a hermit's time of it up here – poor, shattered Bruno.

Anne   Michael.

Michael   Anne?

Bruno   And?

Michael   You're living it up on little old Iona. Bruno the hermit is a fiction.

Anne   Michael.

Michael   Anne?

George   I think . . .

Bruno   What do you think?

Mouse   That was a bit sharp.

Bruno   Don't do that.

Mouse   I was only . . .

Bruno   Don't presume an authority. I'm not in your flock.

Mouse   But you were and you want to be again.

Bruno   Don't.

Mouse   Which might be why I'm here.

Bruno   Just leave it.

Michael   Anyway. What's the evidence to back up my claim, I hear you all say.

Anne   You're making a fool of yourself, Michael. You know that?

Michael   I insist. Exhibit one. Glo-in-the-dark.

He produces one packet of **Anne***'s condoms.*

Exhibit two. Banana flavour.

He produces the second packet.

Exhibit three. Rib-ticklers.

He produces the third packet.

Seed-catchers.
Lots.

George   God.

Michael   It's all right George, they're only condoms. Put your gloves back on if you're scared of them.

Bruno   Where did you find them, Michael?

Michael   Exhibit three is the most interesting. It has a missing element. One condom gone. Mr Scarrow – an explanation please. Are you more than you seem?

Anne   I can't stand this.

Michael   Different language, Anne.
Don't worry, he can play the game as well as I can.

Bruno   Where did you find them, Michael?

Michael   Ask a question to avoid answering one. Classic sign of guilt. I expected more of you, Bruno.

Bruno   Where?

Michael   The witness is digging his own grave.

Bruno Where?

Michael In the pocket of your coat, Mr Scarrow, in the pocket of your coat.

Anne In the pocket of your coat, Mr Scarrow, in the pocket of your coat. Do you know how you sound? Do you? With your mad fucking . . . chattering. Why can't you talk?

Michael Do you know how *you* sound – darling?

George They're mine. (*Beat.*) I put them there.

Michael In Bruno's pocket? George?

George I had them. I bought them. From the hotel. I was here . . . I was here by myself. I heard you coming . . . it was the first place I could . . . silly.

Michael They're yours? I'm sorry. If I'd known . . .

Anne Well, you didn't.

Bruno Were you pick-pocketing my coat?

Michael I was wearing it. You took mine when you went to St Odhran's.

Lights fade down and up again.

George *and* **Mouse** *alone at the table.*

George I'm sorry.

Mouse It's all right. I know you did it for a reason.

George People will . . .

Mouse It doesn't matter what they think. We know the truth. They can think what they like.

George The truth. Yes.

Mouse You're a good person, George.

George Am I? Is that what you think?
I'm not sure what that is.
You're a bit like it.

Mouse   I try very hard. It's not easy.

George   I know.

She goes to the window.

The sky. It's so big.

Mouse   George?

George   Yes?

Mouse   I really don't mind what you said.

George   Would you say things you didn't mean, Mouse?

Mouse   No.

George   I'm very tired.

Mouse   You should . . .

George   Get some sleep.

She is leaving.

Pray for me.

Scene Four

The garden. **Bruno** *and* **Michael**.

Michael   Do you remember the rat we found?

Bruno   There's something I have to tell you.

Michael   Best funeral a rat ever had.

Bruno   I remember.

Michael   Torches flashing. You, pushing the burning raft out into the stream in the middle of the night.

Bruno   It's something you have to listen to, Michael.

Michael   What? Don't tell me. You're screwing my wife.

Bruno   Yes.

Michael   Small boys wept. Shivering in their dressing-gowns.

Bruno   They were cold.

Michael   I wasn't.

Bruno   Nor was I.
And there's a possibility I'm falling in love with her.

Michael   A possibility. Yes. What do you want? My permission?

Bruno   I wanted to tell you.

Michael   And when are you going to decide . . . whether you'll allow yourself to . . . fall in love with my wife?

Pause.

You do want my permission. Don't you? Bruno?

Bruno   I don't know. I wanted to tell you.

Michael   And when all the other boys had gone . . . and the rat in the raft had disappeared, you held my hand and I held yours and both of us cried. Remember? Sobbed and sobbed . . . and never mentioned it again.

Bruno   I remember.

Michael   I remember. Please don't. Please don't, Bruno.

Scene Five

Night. Enter **Anne**. *She is naked. She stands still centre-stage staring straight ahead.*

Enter **George** *carrying a blanket.* **George** *puts the blanket around* **Anne**.

Anne   No! No! No! No!

Scene Six

Morning. The beach. **Bruno** *stands alone looking out to sea.*

Enter **Mouse**.

Mouse   Hello, Bruno.

Bruno   You're going to see the boy.

Mouse   Yes.

Bruno   He's there.

Mouse   Good. It's good to be up early – in a place like this.

Bruno   The hard life.

Mouse   Pardon?

Bruno   A good clean game. Oatcakes and water and pillows made of wood.

Mouse   It can't have been an accident you coming here. Are you staying?

Bruno   Look at the water. Have you ever seen such clear water? Where the pools are bright and deep.

Mouse   Is that something?

Bruno   Something. A poem about boyhood. No one says 'boyhood' any more. He had a difficult boyhood.

Mouse   I do. You destroyed mine.
I've never really told anyone. Why do you think that is?

Bruno   Martyr-Mouse.
What have you said to him?

Mouse   The boy? I'm talking to him about God.

Bruno   Are you? How do you know he doesn't have God already?

Mouse   Because God requires more than silence.

Bruno
    Climb every mountain.
    Ford every stream.
    Follow every rainbow.
    Shout it from the roof-tops.
Do you know how hard it is to hide from all the shouting?

Mouse   I do understand your anger, Bruno.

Bruno   No. You *see* it. You *see* that I am angry and you *see* that it is justified. You do not understand it.

Mouse   I used to lie awake. Waiting.
You shouldn't make a career out of suffering. It doesn't help. You've had your shining moment, Bruno, which is more than I've had. You invited me here . . .

Bruno   To look at.

Mouse   For a purpose. You miss her – Sonia – and you miss what she taught you. You can have her back if you remember what she taught you.

Bruno   I don't believe in you.

Mouse   You invited me here.

Bruno   I don't believe a word you say. You're a weak man. You've made yourself vulnerable becoming what you are. Priest. I don't believe you are strong enough.

Mouse   I have to go – the boy. He's expecting me.
Do it through me, Bruno. Look at me and come back through me.

He takes hold of **Bruno** *by the arm.*

Look me in the eyes. Say to me that you will try. For me.

Bruno   I'm watching you. I'll be watching you.

Scene Seven

The same morning. The cottage. **Anne** *is asleep in a chair with her coat on and the blanket over her.* **Michael** *is sitting at the table.* **Anne** *wakes up.*

Michael   The last time you woke up in a chair in a man's house with a blanket around you it was my chair and my house and my blanket . . .

Anne   Michael.

Michael   The second of June 1979. It was raining.

Anne   It's cold.

Michael   Two days later you finally slipped between my sheets. The fourth of June. It was still raining.

Anne   Was it?

Michael   In those days . . . in the old days . . .

Anne   Yes, Michael.

Michael   In the old days you couldn't look anyone in the eye.

Anne   I'm cold.

Michael   You couldn't even look me in the eye.

Anne   And now I can.

Michael   Do you remember what I said to you the first night?

Anne   Yes.

Michael   Around two o'clock in the morning on the fifth of June, I said I would never go to sleep before you. (*Beat.*) You were so funny and gauche. Funny Anne. And now all polish and spit.

Anne   What time is it? It's late, isn't it?

Michael   Where have you been?

Anne   I don't know.

Michael   Really?

Anne   What is the point of all this, Michael?

Michael   '. . . he forever wed his perishable breath to her unutterable vision.'

Anne   Is everyone up?

Michael   Up and out. It's just the two of us. They all crept out, one by one, smiling at the sleeping beauty. The summer we met . . .

Anne   Yes, Michael?

Michael   We went for a picnic in St James's Park.

Anne   I know. I was there.

Michael   And you picked a daisy and gave it to me – all solemn, eyes down – I kept it – you don't know this – I kept it pressed between page one hundred and sixteen and one hundred and seventeen of my copy of *The Great Gatsby*. A daisy from my Daisy.

Anne   You're getting pathetic.

Michael   Is that what you call it?

Anne   Foolish and sentimental and self-pitying.

Michael   'And so we beat one, boats against the current, borne back ceaselessly into the past.'

Anne   Could you get me my shoes?

Michael   We were happy.

Anne   Yes, we were happy and now we're not happy. What do you want me to do? (*Beat.*) Don't go quiet. You wanted this. You sat there and waited for me to . . . it's not fair to stop.

Michael   Fair? Fair?

Anne   Michael. Don't you understand? There is no high ground left to claim. You know, don't you?

Michael   He told me.

Anne   It wasn't meant to be him.
I'm sorry.

Michael   But it was him, it had to be him. Is it because I can't . . .

Anne   Yes. Partly.

Michael *goes to the window.*

Anne   You asked me. You asked me the question.

Michael   Tell me about it. I want to know. Was it once?

Anne   I'm not going to talk about it.

Michael   I've a right to know.

Anne   I'm not interested in seeing you punish yourself.

Michael   When? When was it?

He sits back at table.

Anne   I'm not going to tell you.

Michael *suddenly swipes at the cups on the table sending them flying.*

Michael   You're not going to tell me!
You're not going to tell me.

Anne *gets her shoes and starts to put them on.*

Michael   What are you doing?

Anne   I'm going out.

Michael   You can't. You've got to talk to me. Anne. Anne.

Anne *is lacing up her shoes.* **Michael** *goes over to her.*

Michael   We have to talk.

Anne *continues lacing up her shoes.*

Michael   Anne.

He kneels and tries to stop her lacing her shoes.

Please. Anne. Please.

Anne *(standing up)*   Where is he?

Michael   You're not even going to talk to me. Do I mean that little? Do I?

He goes to the outside door and stands in front of it.

I won't let you go.

Enter **George**.

George   Sorry. Am I . . . ?

Anne   It's all right. We were talking.

George   I was looking for Mouse.

Michael   He went out.

George   To see the Wallace boy?

Michael   Yes. To see the Wallace boy.

George   How long ago did he . . .

Michael   Early.

George   And Bruno?

Beat.

Anne   Michael?

Michael   I don't know.

Anne   You said you'd seen him?

George   Is he with Mouse?

Anne   Are you all right, George?

George   I think so. I've been . . . the wind . . . it makes you light-headed.

She sits down and looks at **Anne**.

You look funny. You look very funny.

She starts to laugh and then to cry.

Anne (*comforting her*)   It's all right, George. It's all right. Sssh. Sssh. What is it?

George   I'm scared.

Anne   What of?

George   He's a good man.

Anne   Of course he is. No one says . . .

George   I love him. And I'm so frightened.

Anne   That's a part of it. It's one of the things that happens. It's a wonderful thing.

George   I don't mean . . . it's something else . . .

Anne   What is it?

George   Bruno told me . . .

Anne   Bruno?

George   He told me . . . He loves me I think. He can't say it but when I look at him . . .

Michael   What did Bruno say?

Anne   Whatever it is it doesn't matter.

Michael   What did he say?

Anne   You don't have to tell us.

George   He said Mouse had done terrible things. He said he had done things . . . He said . . . (*She breaks down.*) Children. Children. Children.

Anne *holds her.*

Michael   If he said it, it's true.

Anne   Shut up, Michael.

Michael   If he said it, it's true.

Anne   Shut up, Michael.

Michael   He doesn't lie.

Anne *goes to* **Michael**.

Anne   Shut up.

Michael   No. You fucking shut up. Stop dancing round things. With all your sharp edges and clever . . .

Anne   Be quiet.

Michael   George. Listen to me.

He takes **George** *by the arms.* **Anne** *tries to come in between them and he pushes her away.* **George** *is crying quietly.*

Listen to me. If Bruno said it, it's true.

Anne *hits* **Michael** *hard across the face.*

Michael   It's true. It's true.

Anne *rushes out.*

George   No!

Scene Eight

Beach.

Bruno   You've found it, haven't you? My place under the cliff. I can tell. There are mouse droppings all over the place. The monks went there. St Columba himself. Don't you think? Don't you reckon? Imagine.

Mouse   Yes.

Bruno Unbelievable. To sit in the presence of a saint. You can sniff his essence. He scratched his head, he itched his pubic hairs. The dandruff of a saint in the earth beneath you. A thousand tiny white relics, the scalp dust of holy contemplation. Amazing. Hey, Mouse? You've been there all right, tossing and turning, pulling your hair. I can sniff your essence too.

Mouse That day . . . in Regent's Park that day . . . I was looking for someone.

Bruno Yes, Mouse.

Mouse One morning, some months before you found me I was walking in the park and I noticed that the hedge next to me was full of plastic – old food containers, that kind of thing, every ten feet or so. At first I thought it was litter but then I saw that there were birds eating out of them. Someone had put the containers into the hedge to fill with food for the birds. The next time I was in the park I saw her, loading up her containers. She didn't want to be seen – every time she got to one of her spots in the hedge she looked over her shoulder to check . . . to check what? This woman spent her life putting food into plastic containers in a hedge. What can you say about that? What is there to say?

Bruno What do *you* say Mouse?

Mouse I went back to the park many times but I didn't see her. I knew she was still at it because the birds were feeding. Then one day, it was cold I remember, there was snow on the ground, I found her again. She was sitting by the side of the road, the cars had to take the corner carefully so as not to run over her legs. She looked up at me and I saw that she had been crying. I asked her what the matter was and she lifted up her sweater – she had nothing on underneath it – there, lying against her stomach was a very tiny, dead bird. She let me see it and then pulled her sweater down again. What could I say? What can be said about a thing like that?

Bruno What are you saying to me, Mouse?

Mouse I woke up in the middle of the night – I'd fallen asleep in a chair – and it was all very clear to me. What this woman did made her happy and it made her sad and it made her sit down at the side of the road and weep into the snow. I've never had any of those things. All I can manage . . . all I can do is feel sorry for myself. Do you see? Do you?

Beat.

The next time I saw her was a week or so later. I smiled at her and said something and she looked straight through me and moved to the next spot in the hedge. It's what I deserve. Nothing more.

Bruno I agree.

Mouse We are a little alike, you and I.

Bruno But we made our own choices.

Mouse You made me into this.

Bruno Where's the boy?

Mouse He was here.

Bruno Where is he now?

Mouse He won't speak. He never speaks. I held him. I wanted to keep him close to me. It's cold in the mornings.

Bruno What happened?

Mouse I don't know. Oh, God. I don't know. He was here . . . so small . . . I just wanted to hold him. What am I going to do?

Bruno I'm the last person to answer that.

Mouse It was you. You've made all of this happen. It was you.

Bruno We make our own choices. You weren't strong enough.

Mouse   You have to help me. You started it all. You can't leave me.

Bruno   Do you want to know his name. The boy who can't speak. The boy who couldn't say no. Do you even want to know his name?

Mouse (*beat*)   No.

Bruno   The running of the waves, St Columba said, the peace of the running of the waves. Listen to them, Mouse, listen to the running of the waves. What do they tell you? I'll leave you to it. Listen. Listen, man of God. Listen for me.

Exit **Bruno**.

Scene Nine

St Odhran's.

Anne   You're here. Treading on people's graves.

Bruno   Do you see the pathway? It used to run all the way down to the beach. It's called the street of the dead. The dead were carried up from the boats for burial here. You can still get down. If you know your way.

Anne   What's happened?

Bruno   You're out of breath. Have you seen Wallace?

Anne   No.

Bruno   He comes this way about now.

Anne   Is it the boy?

Bruno   I don't know. I'm watching.
Columba died at midnight. He knew when he woke in the morning that it was his deathday. Do you think it was raining that day? Some Iona rain.

Anne   I don't know.

Bruno   Do you think he yawned that morning? Do you think he coughed a little? Did he whisper something up on the hill in the middle of the day? Did he smile inwardly at something no one else saw but him?

Anne   What are you doing?

Bruno   There was a white horse that pulled a cart for the monks. Columba said goodbye to the horse. Imagine.

Anne   Bruno.

Bruno   The horse wept into Columba's lap and the monk who was with them tried to pull the horse away. 'Let him cry. He loves me,' Columba said. Can you imagine? The horse loves me. Let him cry.

Anne   Where is Mouse? Is he on the beach?

Bruno   It will be dark soon.

Anne   George said something.

Bruno   Why are you telling me?

Anne   Do you know what she said?

Bruno   I can guess.

Anne   Bruno. Have you seen Mouse?

Bruno   He's out there. Contemplating.

Anne   Where?

Bruno   The place I go.

Anne   When it gets dark . . .

Bruno   You can't see the join. Do you think the sea comes up to the sky or is it the other way around?

Anne   Look at me.

Bruno   I can't.

Anne   I don't care.

Bruno   All the same, I can't.

Anne   You haven't tried hard enough.

Bruno   With you.

Anne   You could try much harder.

Bruno (*beat*)   It's time to go. Forty minutes out.

Anne   Where are we going?

Bruno   To the hole. To get closer. To look.

He starts to go.

Anne   Bruno? I'm here. I'll be here.

Bruno   I know. (*Beat.*) I did try.

Anne   Look at me.

He doesn't.

Look at me. Please.

Exit **Bruno**. **Anne** *stands alone for some moments. Enter* **George**.

George   I can't find him.

Anne   There. With the boy beside him. On the beach. He's coming back.

George   From where?

Anne   Contemplation over. He's made his choice. He's coming back.

George *makes as if to go.*

Anne   Don't. We should wait. We can watch for the joining. You missed it, didn't you?

George   Bruno. He's going to meet Mouse. (*Beat.*) They passed each other. And they didn't speak.

Anne   They're changing places.

George   They didn't say a word to each other.

Michael (*off*)   Bruno Scarrow. Bruno Scarrow. Bruno Scarrow.

Anne   Look how small he seems. Smaller and smaller, like a little boy. (*Beat.*) The day I came here I found a flower rooted in the sand, about where he is now . . . the only flower on the beach, the strangest thing. Do you think he'll see it? George? Do you think he'll see it and smile to himself? Foolish, delicate flower. Tread lightly, Bruno Scarrow, tread lightly.

George   I can't see him any more.

Anne   Watch. Watch for the joining.

George   There.

Anne   Yes. There. Now.

A silence.

George   He's gone.

Anne   Listen. Do you hear? I can hear him smiling. Do you hear it?

Scene Ten

Michael *and* **Anne**. *The cottage. There is an open suitcase on the table.*

Michael   Do you think he'd mind?

Anne   What is it?

Michael   His copy of *King Lear*.

Anne   You should know.

Michael   I'll take it.

Anne   Something to remember him by.

Michael   He's written in the back.

Anne   What does it say?

Michael   It says: Goneril or Regan. Who's got the biggest tits. Discuss. It all came back, Anne. I mean, it was the same sound.

Anne   Was it?

Michael (*beat*)   What are we going to do?

Anne   What can we do? Pack up and go.

Michael   I meant . . . me and you.

Anne   I think we should be elsewhere . . . to talk about that. Not here.

Michael   You should have something.

Anne   I don't think I want anything.

Michael   I wouldn't mind. I'd understand. If you wanted something.

Anne   No.

Enter **George** *in coat with case in hand.*

George   It was over before we got here. You do know that? We were witnesses. He was finished.

Anne   Is that what you really think?

George   He wanted us to fail.

Anne   I looked into his face. Just once. But a good long time . . . at Bruno Scarrow. He didn't want us to fail.

Enter **Mouse** *in his coat.*

He let us all have a look. Mouse. You had a good, long look all of your own. Tell them. He could have been saved. It's what he wanted.

Mouse (*long beat*)   Yes.

George   Then he was asking too much.

Mouse   He was asking for strength from one of us. Me in particular. I wasn't strong enough. None of us . . .

Michael   Stop.

Anne   Michael.

Michael   Stop talking. Stop. He's dead. He died. Yesterday. For fuck's sake. He waited in his stupid hole for the sea to swallow him up. In the dark. For fuck's sake. That's all now.

Anne   He would have wanted . . .

Michael   What? What would he have wanted?

Anne   . . . us to try and make sense of it.

Michael   He drowned in a stupid miserable hole. That's it. Bruno is dead. Can't you see? Leave him alone. All of you. He needs to be left alone.

A silence.

George   We should go.

Mouse   Yes.

George   Perhaps . . .

Mouse   We were saying . . . we should all meet up . . . soon . . .

Anne   Yes.

Mouse   Michael.

Exit **George** *and* **Mouse**.

Michael *goes suddenly to the record-player and puts on the Sandie Shaw record. 'Always Something There to Remind Me'. He is crying and trying to take his boots off. Finally he stands to attention.* **Anne** *lifts the needle off the record-player.*

Anne   We should stay for a while.

She goes to him and holds him.

METHUEN SCREENPLAYS

☐ BEAUTIFUL THING	Jonathan Harvey	£6.99
☐ THE ENGLISH PATIENT	Anthony Minghella	£7.99
☐ THE CRUCIBLE	Arthur Miller	£6.99
☐ THE WIND IN THE WILLOWS	Terry Jones	£7.99
☐ PERSUASION	Jane Austen, adapted by Nick Dear	£6.99
☐ TWELFTH NIGHT	Shakespeare, adapted by Trevor Nunn	£7.99
☐ THE KRAYS	Philip Ridley	£7.99
☐ THE AMERICAN DREAMS (THE REFLECTING SKIN & THE PASSION OF DARKLY NOON)	Philip Ridley	£8.99
☐ MRS BROWN	Jeremy Brock	£7.99
☐ THE GAMBLER	Dostoyevsky, adapted by Nick Dear	£7.99
☐ TROJAN EDDIE	Billy Roche	£7.99
☐ THE WINGS OF THE DOVE	Hossein Amini	£7.99
☐ THE ACID HOUSE TRILOGY	Irvine Welsh	£8.99
☐ THE LONG GOOD FRIDAY	Barrie Keeffe	£6.99
☐ SLING BLADE	Billy Bob Thornton	£7.99

- All Methuen Drama books are available through mail order or from your local bookshop.

Please send cheque/eurocheque/postal order (sterling only) Access, Visa, Mastercard, Diners Card, Switch or Amex.

☐☐☐☐☐☐☐☐☐☐☐☐☐☐☐

Expiry Date: _____ Signature: _____

Please allow 75 pence per book for post and packing U.K.
Overseas customers please allow £1.00 per copy for post and packing.

ALL ORDERS TO:

Methuen Books, Books by Post, TBS Limited, The Book Service, Colchester Road, Frating Green, Colchester, Essex CO7 7DW.

NAME: _____

ADDRESS: _____

_____

_____

Please allow 28 days for delivery. Please tick box if you do not wish to receive any additional information ☐

Prices and availability subject to change without notice.

METHUEN DRAMA
MONOLOGUE & SCENE BOOKS

☐ CONTEMPORARY SCENES FOR ACTORS (MEN)	Earley and Keil	£8.99
☐ CONTEMPORARY SCENES FOR ACTORS (WOMEN)	Earley and Keil	£8.99
☐ THE CLASSICAL MONOLOGUE (MEN)	Earley and Keil	£7.99
☐ THE CLASSICAL MONOLOGUE (WOMEN)	Earley and Keil	£7.99
☐ THE CONTEMPORARY MONOLOGUE (MEN)	Earley and Keil	£7.99
☐ THE CONTEMPORARY MONOLOGUE (WOMEN)	Earley and Keil	£7.99
☐ THE MODERN MONOLOGUE (MEN)	Earley and Keil	£7.99
☐ THE MODERN MONOLOGUE (WOMEN)	Earley and Keil	£7.99
☐ THE METHUEN AUDITION BOOK FOR MEN	Annika Bluhm	£6.99
☐ THE METHUEN AUDITION BOOK FOR WOMEN	Annika Bluhm	£6.99
☐ THE METHUEN AUDITION BOOK FOR YOUNG ACTORS	Anne Harvey	£6.99
☐ THE METHUEN BOOK OF DUOLOGUES FOR YOUNG ACTORS	Anne Harvey	£6.99

• All Methuen Drama books are available through mail order or from your local bookshop.

Please send cheque/eurocheque/postal order (sterling only) Access, Visa, Mastercard, Diners Card, Switch or Amex.

☐☐☐☐☐☐☐☐☐☐☐☐☐☐☐☐

Expiry Date: _____ Signature: _____

Please allow 75 pence per book for post and packing U.K.
Overseas customers please allow £1.00 per copy for post and packing.

ALL ORDERS TO:

Methuen Books, Books by Post, TBS Limited, The Book Service, Colchester Road, Frating Green, Colchester, Essex CO7 7DW.

NAME: _____

ADDRESS: _____

_____

_____

Please allow 28 days for delivery. Please tick box if you do not wish to receive any additional information ☐

Prices and availability subject to change without notice.

METHUEN STUDENT EDITIONS

☐ SERJEANT MUSGRAVE'S DANCE	John Arden	£6.99
☐ CONFUSIONS	Alan Ayckbourn	£5.99
☐ THE ROVER	Aphra Behn	£5.99
☐ LEAR	Edward Bond	£6.99
☐ THE CAUCASIAN CHALK CIRCLE	Bertolt Brecht	£6.99
☐ MOTHER COURAGE AND HER CHILDREN	Bertolt Brecht	£6.99
☐ THE CHERRY ORCHARD	Anton Chekhov	£5.99
☐ TOP GIRLS	Caryl Churchill	£6.99
☐ A TASTE OF HONEY	Shelagh Delaney	£6.99
☐ STRIFE	John Galsworthy	£5.99
☐ ACROSS OKA	Robert Holman	£5.99
☐ A DOLL'S HOUSE	Henrik Ibsen	£5.99
☐ MY MOTHER SAID I NEVER SHOULD	Charlotte Keatley	£6.99
☐ DREAMS OF ANNE FRANK	Bernard Kops	£5.99
☐ BLOOD WEDDING	Federico Lorca	£5.99
☐ THE MALCONTENT	John Marston	£5.99
☐ BLOOD BROTHERS	Willy Russell	£6.99
☐ DEATH AND THE KING'S HORSEMAN	Wole Soyinka	£6.99
☐ THE PLAYBOY OF THE WESTERN WORLD	J.M. Synge	£5.99
☐ OUR COUNTRY'S GOOD	Timberlake Wertenbaker	£6.99
☐ THE IMPORTANCE OF BEING EARNEST	Oscar Wilde	£5.99
☐ A STREETCAR NAMED DESIRE	Tennessee Williams	£5.99

• All Methuen Drama books are available through mail order or from your local bookshop.

Please send cheque/eurocheque/postal order (sterling only) Access, Visa, Mastercard, Diners Card, Switch or Amex.

☐☐☐☐☐☐☐☐☐☐☐☐☐☐☐

Expiry Date: _____ Signature: _____

Please allow 75 pence per book for post and packing U.K.
Overseas customers please allow £1.00 per copy for post and packing.

ALL ORDERS TO:

Methuen Books, Books by Post, TBS Limited, The Book Service, Colchester Road, Frating Green, Colchester, Essex CO7 7DW.

NAME: _____

ADDRESS: _____

_____

Please allow 28 days for delivery. Please tick box if you do not
wish to receive any additional information   ☐

Prices and availability subject to change without notice.

Methuen Contemporary Dramatists
include

Peter Barnes (three volumes)
Sebastian Barry
Edward Bond (six volumes)
Howard Brenton
  (two volumes)
Richard Cameron
Jim Cartwright
Caryl Churchill (two volumes)
Sarah Daniels (two volumes)
David Edgar (three volumes)
Dario Fo (two volumes)
Michael Frayn (two volumes)
Peter Handke
Jonathan Harvey
Declan Hughes
Terry Johnson
Bernard-Marie Koltès
Doug Lucie
David Mamet (three volumes)

Anthony Minghella
  (two volumes)
Tom Murphy (four volumes)
Phyllis Nagy
Peter Nichols (two volumes)
Philip Osment
Louise Page
Stephen Poliakoff
  (three volumes)
Christina Reid
Philip Ridley
Willy Russell
Ntozake Shange
Sam Shepard (two volumes)
David Storey (three volumes)
Sue Townsend
Michel Vinaver (two volumes)
Michael Wilcox

Methuen World Classics
include

Jean Anouilh (two volumes)
John Arden (two volumes)
Arden & D'Arcy
Brendan Behan
Aphra Behn
Bertolt Brecht (six volumes)
Büchner
Bulgakov
Calderón
Anton Chekhov
Noël Coward (five volumes)
Eduardo De Filippo
Max Frisch
Gorky
Harley Granville Barker
 (two volumes)
Henrik Ibsen (six volumes)
Lorca (three volumes)
Marivaux

Mustapha Matura
David Mercer (two volumes)
Arthur Miller (five volumes)
Molière
Musset
Clifford Odets
Joe Orton
A. W. Pinero
Luigi Pirandello
Terence Rattigan
W. Somerset Maugham
 (two volumes)
Wole Soyinka
August Strindberg
 (three volumes)
J. M. Synge
Ramón del Valle-Inclán
Frank Wedekind
Oscar Wilde

Methuen Classical Greek Dramatists

Aeschylus Plays: One
(Persians, Seven Against Thebes, Suppliants,
Prometheus Bound)

Aeschylus Plays: Two
(Oresteia: Agamemnon, Libation-Bearers, Eumenides)

Aristophanes Plays: One
(Acharnians, Knights, Peace, Lysistrata)

Aristophanes Plays: Two
(Wasps, Clouds, Birds, Festival Time, Frogs)

Aristophanes & Menander: New Comedy
(Women in Power, Wealth, The Malcontent,
The Woman from Samos)

Euripides Plays: One
(Medea, The Phoenician Women, Bacchae)

Euripides Plays: Two
(Hecuba, The Women of Troy, Iphigeneia at Aulis,
Cyclops)

Euripides Plays: Three
(Alkestis, Helen, Ion)

Euripides Plays: Four
(Elektra, Orestes, Iphigeneia in Tauris)

Euripides Plays: Five
(Andromache, Herakles' Children, Herakles)

Euripides Plays: Six
(Hippolytos, Suppliants, Rhesos)

Sophocles Plays: One
(Oedipus the King, Oedipus at Colonus, Antigone)

Sophocles Plays: Two
(Ajax, Women of Trachis, Electra, Philoctetes)

For a Complete Catalogue of Methuen Drama titles
write to:

Methuen Drama
215 Vauxhall Bridge Road
London SW1V 1EJ